Cogn... Behavioral Therapy

The 21 Day CBT Workbook For Overcoming Fear, Anxiety And Depression

How To Use 30 Proven Techniques To Get Measurable Relief And Improve Your Daily Life

Jacob Greene

Table of Contents

Introduction

Problems.

That is a definite common denominator for everyone on planet earth. Whatever we want to coin it as – challenges, milestones, issues, and a whole myriad of other colorful terms. One thing is for certain. Everyone would have problems. Problems of the material sort, problems stemming from the mind and emotions. The question here is what would you choose to do when faced with them?

For the issues that originate from the mind and emotion, the contents of this book would be well suited to help you with tackling those matters. For folks suffering from phobias, anxiety as well as the more common than thought incidences of depression, the good news is that you can be empowered with the right tools contained within this book to help with handling those issues.

So much of our lives is determined by our thoughts and emotions. Even the most rational and logical of us would sometimes let our hearts rule over our heads. They say that the secret to the Universe is this: our thoughts shape our realities. We attract what we think, and through our thoughts, we manifest what we fixate on.

This means that if you're a pessimist who always sees the negative side of things, you'll only attract more negativity into your life; whereas optimists are positive thinkers who are grateful for everything that comes their way, and in doing so, multiply their blessings and become more abundant in goodness.

Whether you believe in the magic of the Universe or not, the power of our thoughts and the actions they invoke in us is undeniable. Just imagine what you could do if you had complete, masterful control over your own thoughts, actions, and emotions. The possibilities would be limitless. This is why Cognitive-Behavioral Therapy (CBT) matters so much.

The guiding principle behind CBT is that our thoughts determine our feelings and behaviors, and so, in gaining better control over your mind, you will be able to change the way you feel and the things you do. It might seem like common sense, but it's actually harder than you think. Have you ever done something you knew you shouldn't have but couldn't stop yourself from, like lying or yelling at a loved one? Or tried to quit a bad habit like smoking or gambling, but found yourself struggling to do so? It's easier said than done, right?

Never underestimate the power of your thoughts. Positive thoughts can do so much to make your life better; it can lift your spirits and boost your confidence, making it easier to connect with others and enjoy yourself. On the other hand, negative thoughts can do a lot to harm us and our self-esteem. Over thinking, being pessimistic and worrying too much can cause us anxiety, fear, and if left unchecked, lead us to depression. A lot of the mental and emotional issues we struggle with are actually rooted in negative thinking and pessimistic beliefs. This is where CBT comes into play.

While there are many other kinds of therapy readily available to us right now, none have been quite as popular as CBT, largely thanks to its easy application and simple techniques. It integrates both behavioral and cognitive theories of psychology and targets our unrealistic thoughts and faulty ways of thinking, which distort our views and attitudes towards ourselves, our circumstances, and the world around us, and corrects them to help us become more emotionally and mentally well-adjusted.

All too often our problems and personal struggles stem from a negative view of ourselves and our situation. Our distorted thinking leads us to misinterpret things for the worse and makes it harder for us to cope with our stress and the challenges we face. With the help of CBT, you can finally learn how to overcome your anxiety, fears & phobias, obsessive thinking, and depression.

In this book, you will find a 21-day step-by-step program that will teach you all about Cognitive-Behavioral Therapy and how to practice it in your everyday life. It will show you over 30 different ways you can use CBT to overcome the hardships you face with simple, easy, and reliable tips and techniques.

However, it is by no means a perfect and absolute solution to all your problems. It can't cure your depression or rid you of your mental illness permanently and completely, but it can do a lot to make it more manageable, grant you relief, and improve your overall quality of life.

When I was a young boy, I was diagnosed with attention-deficit hyperactivity disorder (ADHD) and it's something I constantly struggled with, growing up. Because it was so hard for me to concentrate, I often did poorly in school and failed a lot of my classes. It was hard for me to make friends because everyone thought I talked too much to carry a normal conversation and no one could understand or empathize with my condition.

I felt embarrassed about my ADHD and I hated how it made me feel so isolated from everyone else, like I was going too fast and forever waiting for someone to catch up to me. I can't count the number of times I wished I had an "off" button for my brain, just so I could stop feeling stupid or different or wrong. So believe me when I say that I know what it's like to struggle with mental illness.

But then, after I started seeking therapy and counseling, I discovered cognitive-behavioral therapy, and it did wonders for me. Life got so much better once I started practicing CBT, so much so that I was intrigued enough to research about it some more and learn as much as I could so I could help others like me. Now here I am, writing this book.

So if you're ready to start living your best life today and want to learn how to better control your own thoughts, feelings, and actions, then come and join me on my journey to mental wellness through CBT.

Chapter 1: CBT 101

The History of CBT

One of the leading forms of psychosocial intervention practiced by many counselors and mental health professionals of today, Cognitive-Behavioral Therapy (CBT) is a psychotherapeutic treatment that aims to help patients understand and control the thoughts and feelings which influence their behaviors, and ultimately, overcome the destructive behavioral patterns that result from their negative thinking and unrealistic beliefs.

As you might have already surmised from its name, CBT came about after rise and fall of both cognitive and behavioral theories of psychology. A brainchild of the 1960s, it emerged as the solution that addressed the criticisms and shortcomings of the two fields and integrated them into a single, cohesive practice.

The theoretical roots of CBT can be traced back as early as 1913, during the beginnings of behaviorism as pioneered by John B. Watson whose work laid the foundation for a lot of CBT's concepts. After that, it was also heavily influenced by the work of Albert Ellis on Rational Emotive Behavioral Therapy (REBT) in the 1950s as well.

With that said though, it's actually Dr. Aaron T. Beck that most consider to be the formal founder and first pioneer of Cognitive

Behavioral Therapy (CBT). While working as a psychiatrist at the University of Pennsylvania, Beck discovered that the psychotherapy he had been using to treat most of his clients' depression had not been effective and that his experimental findings contradicted and disproved the fundamental concepts of Freud's psychoanalytic theory, from which the therapy was based off of.

Instead, what he observed was that most of his clients often had internal experiences (thoughts and feelings) that significantly impacted their behaviors and led them to develop a lot of the psychological distress and mental health problems for which they sought professional help for. This "internal dialogue", as he called it, impacted their perceptions and attitudes towards a certain person or situation in ways many of them did not realize. For example, a previously cooperative client might think to himself, "This is so hard. The therapy isn't working and I'll never get better," and thus, start to become more resistant, despondent, and apathetic towards both the therapist and their condition.

Because of this, Beck started to conceptualize depression in terms of the streams of impulsive, negative thoughts that his depressed patients often struggled (and failed) to overcome. He coined the term "automatic thoughts" to refer to this phenomenon and posited that people interact with the world through their mental representations of it (i.e., thoughts, ideas, belief systems). Thus, if a person's mental representation or reasoning is inaccurate or dysfunctional, then their feelings and behaviors may become problematic.

Realizing the importance of what he had discovered, began developing his own psychological theory and therapy. He investigated the kinds of automatic thoughts that seemed to be most common among his clients and categorized them as: negative ideas about the self; negative beliefs about the world; and negative views of the future.

With this, he got to work on how to identify and correct these automatic thoughts. This emphasis on thought processes was the reason why Beck initially labeled his approach as simply "Cognitive Therapy" instead of "Cognitive-Behavioral Therapy." Later on, however, he would rename it to CBT as he began to borrow heavily from previously established behavioral techniques to treat the negative mentality of his clients.

He helped his patients identify their own automatic thoughts and encouraged them to think more objectively and consider things more realistically. Once they corrected their underlying beliefs, it became easier for clients to stop their maladaptive behaviors and conquer their feelings of depression, anxiety, guilt, trauma, and negativity. This would eventually lead them to emotional relief and allowed them to function better as a whole.

With that said, however, CBT as a field of study has gone beyond the work of Aaron Beck and has now become an umbrella term for many different therapeutic techniques with the same fundamental elements and assumptions.

One example of this is Albert Ellis' Rational Emotive Behavior Therapy (REBT), which we mentioned earlier. Similar to Beck's CBT, REBT is a kind of cognitive therapy that seeks to resolve a client's emotional and behavioral issues through correcting their irrational beliefs. It was from Ellis' work that much of Beck's ideas originated.

Dr. Judith Beck, the daughter of Aaron Beck, is another important proponent of CBT as she did a lot to continue her father's work through her research and development of better CBT techniques. She also encouraged positive coping mechanisms in her clients. Now she is widely regarded as the foremost expert authority on CBT and one of the best and most skilled CBT therapists working today.

Currently, CBT is the most empirically validated and effective form of psychosocial intervention in the world of clinical practice. It has gone on to inspire more than a thousand research papers and has been used to treat a number of mental health problems and psychological disorders. Aside from that, CBT also owes a great deal of its popularity to its success in treating many of society's most prevalent mental disorders, such as eating disorders, anxiety disorders, mood disorders, trauma-related disorders, and more.

With that said, the field has certainly come a long way since it began over half a century ago, and it remains relevant and beneficial to this day. Many experts would agree that Cognitive-Behavioral Therapy (CBT) has undoubtedly become an integral cornerstone not just in clinical psychology and therapy, but in self-help and mental wellness as a whole.

How CBT Can Help

Now that you've been acquainted with a brief history of CBT and how it has developed and changed throughout the years, it's time to move on to the many different ways CBT can help people. Enumerated below are just a few of its many benefits and advantages, such as:

It can solve a specific problem

As we've mentioned before, CBT is actually a general term for a classification of a number of different therapeutic techniques, all of which are guided by the same underlying principle, and that is: when we change our thoughts, we change our lives. This makes CBT an incredibly versatile approach and enables it to address a wide range of issues just by identifying the maladaptive thought or behavior the client would like to correct the most.

For example, someone suffering from anorexia will need to change the way he/she feels about himself/herself and his/her body; whereas a patient struggling with social anxiety must resolve his/her feelings of insecurity and social isolation and target the

10

thoughts that trigger them. These two clients have different presenting problems, but CBT can benefit them both because it can be tailored to fit any problem in particular, so CBT techniques can help just about everyone.

It is goal-oriented

It's been said many times that CBT is a goal-oriented therapy. This means that there is a clear and definitive objective in mind that the client and the therapist must define at the start of their relationship. During every session, they will work towards realizing this goal step by step, and both parties understand what it is that they ultimately want to achieve.

This is an advantage because it clarifies the purpose of the therapy and makes sure that both the therapist and the individual are in agreement about what they are looking to achieve. Sometimes, with other kinds of therapy like psychotherapy or behavioral therapy, this is not the case. In CBT, what the client wants to achieve is often what the therapist will do for them.

It gives the client more freedom

Similar to the previous point, another advantage that CBT has over other psychotherapeutic approaches is that it is more collaborative than most. CBT practitioners often work together with their clients to help them overcome their problems and alleviate their psychological distress. It is directive and focused, but it also allows the client more freedom and control over the therapeutic process.

CBT is also more interactive and requires mutual effort from both parties for the therapy to succeed. The therapist's role is to listen and guide them through their thoughts and experiences; while the client needs to be open, honest, and expressive. So while the counselor's guidance is important, the client's participation and involvement is equally as integral..

It deals with current problems

Unlike other therapeutic approaches, CBT mainly deals with present-day problems and experiences. It addresses thoughts and behavioral patterns that are currently detrimental to the client. It doesn't dig deeper into their past or analyze their childhood experiences and subconscious drives. Rather, it is firmly rooted in the here and now, and it emphasizes the client's current issues at hand.

This is part of the reason why it is the least time-consuming of all the therapeutic approaches, and also a factor for why it is so practical and efficient. Clients can start to see positive results and progress quicker because CBT helps them deal with their issues and improve their current state of mind. It doesn't waste time trying too hard to uncover the deeper or hidden meaning behind things.

It is faster than other forms of therapy

This brings us to the next advantage of CBT: it is a time-limited approach. As stated before, it is the least time-consuming of all the kinds of psychotherapy and takes only one to two months before clients can start to see some progress. On average, most clients will often need 20 hourly sessions on a regular basis, usually once a week, so the therapy can be completed in over five to six months.

This is why CBT is the most recommended form of therapy for clients looking for a simple and effective solution that can alleviate their psychological distress and better enable them to deal with their problems. It is quick and efficient, and most people have a good idea about what to expect.

Moreover, clients can also benefit from CBT in the sense that less sessions means it's less costly. It's a great help for people who are seeking professional help and counseling, but cannot afford to spend more than 6 months in therapy (be it due to time constraints or financial reasons).

It is easily accessible

CBT is perhaps the easiest to understand and apply of all the psychotherapeutic approaches. It's highly structured nature lends itself well to several different mediums, which makes it one of the most accessible and widely available forms of counseling. From individual counseling, to group counseling, to self-help books like this one — almost anyone can learn and practice CBT.

It can help with many different mental health problems

An evidence-based therapy, thousands of studies to date have documented and demonstrated the effectiveness of CBT in dealing with a wide range of mental health problems.

From clinical diagnoses like post-traumatic stress disorder (PTSD), generalized anxiety disorder (GAD), social anxiety disorder, borderline personality disorder, and eating disorders like anorexia nervosa and bulimia; to more common problems like overcoming addiction, recovering from substance abuse, dealing with depression, relationship problems, and anger management — CBT can help with quite a number of things, as you can see.

It helps you grow as a person

When you begin to seek help through CBT, it will promote positive behavioral change and personal growth in you. Through this process, you will be able to identify the root of your problems and understand your role in perpetuating your own unhappiness.

CBT can help you see the impact of your negative thoughts and beliefs, and once you do, you will begin to work towards changing them. This will make you more kind, forgiving, and accepting of yourself and your shortcomings, as you will start to correct your own negative self-concepts.

It will make you more positive

You might remember that earlier ago we said that Dr. Aaron Beck, the founding father of CBT, was able to identify three major kinds of automatic thoughts: negative ideas about the self; negative beliefs about the world; and negative views of the future.

In line with this, CBT is geared towards helping people overcome this negative mindset and instead, encourage them to adopt more beneficial ways of thinking and behaving. In this way, CBT can do a lot to help a person become more positive, as it addresses their negative views of the world and the future.

Cognitive-behavioral therapy (CBT) has the power to transform an individual's way of thinking, so they can replace their negative thought patterns with a more positive outlook on life. Clients will learn to stop jumping to conclusions, stop seeing things as purely all-good or all-bad, stop comparing themselves to others or blaming themselves too harshly for mistakes, and many other different kinds of maladaptive mindsets.

It promotes mental wellness

The main goal of psychotherapy is to promote mental wellness, and CBT is no different. It has countless of different benefits that can do this (many of which we've already named on this list). It can be as effective as medication in treating certain mental health disorders and doesn't put you at risk of dependence or can be helpful in cases where medication alone is not effective.

Other benefits include: helping a person reduce their stress, overcome their past trauma, stop over thinking or ruminating, calming their mind, and learning to regulate their emotions better.

The last part has become a focus of many psychotherapeutic efforts of recent years (such as positive psychology and mindfulness). It's important that a person knows how to control their thoughts and emotions instead of letting it control them.

It makes you more rational
In order for CBT to be successful in treating a client's psychological distress or dysfunction, the person must first learn to be aware of their own maladaptive thoughts in order to correctly identify the root of the problem and resolve it. They can do this through mindfulness training, meditation, and practicing emotional self-awareness, all of which helps them to become more objective and reasonable in their thoughts.

Cognitive-Behavioral Therapy (CBT) teaches your mind to see things from a new perspective and consider the truthfulness of your beliefs. It helps you think more clearly and makes you more resilient against negative thinking and feelings, thus allowing for better judgment and decision-making.

It makes you more empathetic
With the previous point in mind, CBT can also help you to become more empathetic by training you to be more level-headed in dealing with your problems. It encourages you to see past your own point of view and helps you see things better from other people's perspectives. You become better at distinguishing facts from irrational thoughts, and you gain more insight into the motivations behind the actions of others.

The last and most important way that CBT can help a person is by training them to become their own therapist. The ultimate goal of CBT is to guide its clients as they overcome their personal dilemmas and teaches them how to change their perceptions for the better, to see things more clearly and constructively.

It shows us how to approach our psychological distress with calmness and peace of mind, which makes us better equipped to handle negative or stressful situations. Moreover, the ability to resolve our problems on our gives us a better sense of control over our lives and builds our self-esteem and feelings of self-efficacy.

Cognitive-Behavioral Therapy (CBT) instills its clients with better coping strategies to help them deal with a wide variety of everyday challenges and overcome the hardships of life on their own. The skills you can acquire in CBT are useful, practical, and helpful in everyday life. It has also been proven to keep people from relapsing into their old, self-destructive ways and improve their overall quality of life.

Is CBT Right For You?

With all that said, now it's time to ask yourself whether or not trying Cognitive-Behavioral Therapy (CBT) is right for you.

With so many different options available when it comes to counseling and therapy, it's easy to feel confused and not know which one is best for you. Sometimes it's all a matter of trial-and-error, or simply asking your therapist for their professional opinion about which treatment option is suitable for you. However, if you can't afford to do either, then you can at least do some research and try to find out for yourself.

Thankfully, over here most of the research has been done for you. Now all that's left is for you to do some confirmatory checks and ask yourself the following questions:

What is my diagnosis?

Most of the people seeking therapy have been diagnosed with serious mental illnesses, and while it's not entirely necessary, it's best to ask for a psychological assessment from a trained professional to determine whether or not you have one, too.

In a nutshell, most mental illnesses are gauged on the level of the distress they cause the individual; how much they deviate from normal behavior; whether or not they cause significant impairment in a person's social, mental, or emotional functioning; and whether it makes the individual a danger to themselves or others.

Knowing your diagnosis can do a lot to help you figure out which type of psychosocial treatment is best for you. Each mental illness responds differently to each kind of therapy, so you should go for the one that's been proven to be the most effective in treating your specific diagnosis and symptoms.

However, if you don't have a diagnosis or feel that you don't have a serious mental illness, but rather, personal problems that you would just like to resolve, then CBT is the best answer for you. And as we've said many times before, it's also effective in treating anxiety disorders (i.e., GAD, social phobia), eating disorders (i.e., bulimia, anorexia), and mood disorders (i.e., bipolar disorder, major depression).

How serious are my problems?

Similarly to the last question, the seriousness of your mental health problems is an important consideration to whether or not CBT will work best for you. If you suffer from panic attacks, general anxiety, insomnia, specific phobias, substance abuse and addiction, relationship problems, anger management problems, or any of the disorders we've mentioned above, then CBT can help you.

However, if your problems are more severe or complex, then you might need a more long-term treatment plan, especially if you have multiple diagnoses or have a chronic or recurrent mental illness (like a personality disorder or an intellectual disability).

Are my problems rooted in my thoughts?

The fundamental idea behind CBT, as you already know, is that our thoughts direct our behaviors, so it's specially designed to treat problems wherein the individual's automatic thoughts play a crucial role in their problems. With the help of CBT, you will be better able to control and reframe your mindset ("I'm no good, I'm always messing up. Nobody likes me."), which will alleviate your emotional distress and help you eliminate your dysfunctional behaviors.

However, if your problems are not rooted in your thoughts, but rather your environment, physiology, or things that are out of your control, then CBT might not be the best choice for you. Someone suffering at the hands of an abusive partner or family, for example, can only be able change the way he/she feels and responds to the abuse, but still have to live with it. So as long as there is abuse, there will always be some degree of unhappiness in his/her life.

Do I have a clear problem to solve?

CBT is a solution-focused, goal-oriented therapy. Because it's only a short-term process, there needs to be a specific problem that you want to work on resolving. If you want to quit smoking or get over a bad breakup, for example, then CBT is a suitable option for you.

On the other hand, if you're just generally unhappy or dissatisfied with your life but can't think of a particular reason why (i.e., no past trauma, no abuse, no significant failures), CBT might not help.

If you're also interested in exploring your dreams and unconscious memories, or want to understand the meaning of life, then you're better off with psychoanalytic therapy than CBT, because CBT is more practical, direct, and focused on the here and now.

Am I ready to confront my personal issues?

Because you will be spending so much time analyzing and understanding your thoughts, you might learn or recall some uncomfortable things about yourself and your life. You will need to talk about your problems openly with your therapist in order for them to help you, as therapy cannot work if the client isn't ready to be emotionally vulnerable and confront their personal issues.

So before you go on, ask yourself: am I comfortable thinking about my feelings? Can I handle my emotions and my anxiety? It might be a bit upsetting at first, but if you really want to solve your problems, the best way is to face it head-on.

Can I dedicate time to therapy?

Even though CBT is quite a short-term process by most standards, 5-6 months is still a considerable period of time. You will have to go to hourly sessions once a week and sometimes even come home with homework and exercises for you to do outside of these sessions. This can be time-consuming, but you have to commit to the process in order to benefit from it.

Some people go to therapy and don't come back because they feel it wasn't effective or that it wasn't worth the time. People like this often expect therapy to happen overnight, but it doesn't. Not only will you need to dedicate your time to the healing process, but you must be emotionally invested, committed, and motivated as well.

So if you can't dedicate this time to allow yourself to get better and work through your problems patiently, then CBT will not be effective for you.

Do I believe in the power of therapy?
Before you try CBT, be honest with yourself first about whether or not you really believe that it can help you. If you're not at least open to trying it or willing to commit yourself to the process, then therapy is really not for you.

Therapy is a collaborative effort. Your therapist will help you get better, but they're not going to do the work for you. They're only there to guide you and help you through it. You need to be the one who wants to change and actually make an effort to improve your life with more positive thinking and healthier behaviors. If you don't, then you're just wasting your time. There really isn't any magic pill to be the cure-all for the mental distresses that we may face over the course of our lives.

So is CBT really right for you? It's a difficult question to grapple with. In summary, those who will benefit from CBT are generally people who: know what their problem is and want to fix it; are willing to work hard and put in the effort to do so; and know that their issues can be solved with a more positive and constructive mindset.

Getting the Most Out of CBT

After you've pondered on all the questions above and have decided that CBT is the right choice for you, it's time to discuss how you can make the most out of it. Here are a few ways you can do that:

Embrace change

CBT is all about creating positive change in your life through your thoughts. Sometimes change can be hard — maybe even painful — but it's a crucial part of life. Trust in the process, even if you feel a bit of distress or discomfort. You have to understand that sometimes, things can get worse before they get better, just like how it always seems the darkest before dawn.

Set a time table for yourself

It's good to have goals and then set deadlines for yourself on when you want to achieve them. This gives you a sense of urgency and makes you more committed to getting better through CBT.

Be honest with yourself

It can be scary to think about your deepest fears and insecurities, but it can also deliver the best possible results CBT has to offer you. So no matter how painful it may be to think about what you're going through, you need to allow yourself to be completely honest and emotionally vulnerable in order for you to succeed in therapy.

Reflect on what happened

Everything you do in CBT has a purpose, so reflect on it. CBT helps you understand the dysfunctional thoughts, feelings, and behaviors you experience and redirect you towards a better, healthier way of life. Taking the time to ponder on what these problems are will give you a better idea on how to resolve them and enhance your therapeutic experience.

Integrate CBT into your life

Perhaps the best and most effective way to get the most out of CBT is by integrating it into your life. This ensures that, even after this book's 21-day step by step program with CBT is over, it can still create real and lasting change in your life.

You can do this by setting aside some time from your schedule to practice CBT techniques and methods on a regular basis or coming back to them every time you encounter a personal problem. Remember everything you learn here and apply it as often as you can to yourself, your life, and even as advice to others. Only by doing so will you be able to reap all the benefits and rewards of Cognitive-Behavioral Therapy.

Chapter 2: Essential Things You Need To Know About CBT

How CBT Deals with things

Cognitive Behavioral Therapy is a well-known psychotherapy treatment that is notable for its positive results and feedbacks. It has helped thousands of individuals overcome different things and helps them regain control in their lives. It caters to different aspects on how a person responds to a certain situation or problem.

CBT is quite a complex and intricate method to understand. It is composed of several different aspects that should be understood before initiating the process. The three main parts of CBT are: thoughts, emotions and behaviors. These are all interconnected and can significantly impact one another.

Starting off with the chain, thoughts are one of the most crucial and important aspect wherein if negative thoughts are present, it may lead to negative emotions that can also trigger negative behavior. With that being said, everything lies within what the individual's train of thought is and how they deal with it.

Emotions are also crucial since this greatly indicates what and how a person might feel. Behavior deals with how a person interprets their thoughts and emotions and how they want to handle as well as express themselves in any particular situation. In this chain, behavior is mainly dependent on a person's thought and emotion. It deals with the cognitive aspect of a person as well as their behavior.

In terms of their train of thought, individuals will learn on how to accept the current situation they're in and, instead of choosing to think about the negative thoughts and emotions, they learn on how to focus more on the positive aspects in life. They try to see the silver lining in each situation and try to shed light on favorable emotions.

As for the behavioral aspect of CBT, it alters the way that different individuals react to various scenarios. When faced with a problem or situation, CBT allows them to take control of how they might behave and respond to it and lets them be a better person.

There are many different methods and tools of CBT. This type of treatment can be found in health centers wherein professionals can lead you through a rigorous process and help you on your way to wellness.

Some techniques in CBT include the following:

Cognitive Restructuring

Cognitive Restructuring is a common CBT exercise that can significantly aid individuals in dealing with their problems. This addresses the way an individual processes their thoughts and ultimately affects the emotions and behavior that follow.

How does it work? Well, CBT is specifically designed to allow individuals to recognize unfavorable thought patterns and find a way to alter them. Through this, it ultimately reconstructs the emotional system and gradually works through a person's depression, anxiety and other emotional and behavioral disorders. It involves identifying all the beliefs and ideas in one's mind and separates the positive from the negative ones.

Next to that, it assesses the unfavorable ideas and tries to turn it into favorable concepts. How? Negative ideas stem from over-thinking or reading too much into a situation. Through Cognitive Restructuring, it finds a silver lining under every situation and sticks to the positive side of everything. Unfavorable thoughts are eliminated and put to rest by replacing them with positive ideas that can essentially help the individual in the long run.

Cognitive Restructuring alters the ideas that a person thinks about when reacting to a situation from negative ones to positive ideas. The way an individual thinks in response to a situation will be turned into favorable ones by identifying unfavorable thought patterns then finding a positive alternative for this.

This can be done in a lot of different ways. First, individuals need to find general and automatic thoughts that are instantly recurring in our everyday experience. Then, we have to assess these thoughts if ever they are actually true and figure out if they are healthy or negative ideas.

Once they have made a decision, the individual has to replace these automatic thoughts with positive ones if ever they are negative in the first place, or keep these thoughts if they are creating good and positive impact in your life. When replacing them, they must create a better and much more favorable point of view that can essentially benefit them. Through this, they can create a good solution to eliminate the item that has been causing them distress.

For a clearer view of the process, let us start with an example. Say, a depressed person is often pessimistic and has little hope in life. This is a result from a negative loop between their negative thoughts which lead to negative emotions that produce negative behavior than can ultimately lead to other negative ideas and repeat the cycle again. This can be a problem for them to connect with other people and do normal things that can possibly lighten up their mood. With CBT, it works directly at the initial stage of the process and helps them alter their negative thoughts into positive ones to create a positive outlook for them. Ultimately, it can help depressed individuals become much more optimistic in life and have a little hope for the things to come.

Mindfulness Meditation

Meditation is practice that allows an individual to attain mental and emotional clarity. This technique uses strategies like mindfulness, breathing exercises, and self-awareness. Meditation can be done in a lot of different ways.

With that being said, there are several known types of meditation, each catering to a specific aspect that can essentially promote a clearer mind and soul. Breath awareness meditation pays attention to mindful breathing. This helps the individual focus more on the way they breathe and disregards all the thoughts that enter their mind. It benefits the individual by minimizing anxiety, worry, greater concentration and a better emotional state.

There are also other types such as Zen Meditation, Transcendental Meditation and Loving-kindness Meditation that can ultimately help individuals arrive at a clearer mind set and better soul.

Focusing more on mindfulness meditation, this particular type of meditation is also recognized to be an effective technique in promoting cognitive behavioral therapy. It can be used as a tool in aiding problems within the cognitive and behavioral aspect. Mindfulness is a type of meditation that coaxes individuals to be aware of the things happening within the present time and become more vigilant of their surroundings. This entirely disregards the past and focuses on the events we have at hand. It dictates that the present surroundings are the only things that matters.

This unique type of meditation can be practiced anywhere, at any time of the day. As an illustration, when individuals are waiting for a long line to purchase something or waiting for the bus at the bus stop, they can easily take note of everything that is currently happening around them. They become more aware of the things that surround them such as the different people, sounds and smell. They perceive what their senses perceive.

Mindfulness can be found in a majority of the meditation techniques. It can be extremely helpful in focusing on different matters. Breath awareness meditation is one example of where mindfulness is also incorporated.

Mindfulness meditation is known to be a great treatment for a lot of psychological problems, ranging from depression to anxiety and PTSDs. The benefits of mindfulness meditation includes lower fixation of unfavorable thoughts and emotions, better focus, sharper memory, reduced impulsive reactions and satisfaction in relationships. Mindfulness meditation can promote CBT because it also alters the way the brain works and how it processes information. It can reduce negative emotions, as what CBT also does, and boost positive ones to take their place. It lessens anxiety and helps us to change the manner we behave in certain situations to make us be better. Through mindfulness meditation, not only will the individual's mental health be enhanced but as well as their physical structure too.

Mindfulness pays closer attention to thoughts and emotions which are actually the 2 main and crucial aspects of CBT. Since it promotes a positive and desirable outcome for an individual's train of thought, it will most likely result to favorable emotions and better behavior.

Graded/ Gradual Exposure

Another viable technique for Cognitive Behavioral Therapy that individuals may utilize is graded/gradual exposure. This exercise is specially created with the intention of reducing fear and anxiety by slowly and progressively facing them and coming in contact with that object, place, situation or person. Graded/Gradual Exposure is actually perceived to be one of the most common and effective methods to take in overcoming a certain psychological problem. Professionals from all over the world have the same favorable results regarding this treatment and can say that it has really helped multiple individuals around the globe in coming to terms with the things they fear the most.

So, here's the story. Individuals tend to avoid the things they don't want or fear the most. As a result, their fear of that particular object, place, person or situation will only increase as they think about it. However, if they try to expose themselves to that particular fear in a gradual manner, they may be less inclined to fear it. This will slowly reduce their fear for that certain matter until will ultimately disappear.

To better understand it, here's an example. A person who is extremely afraid of being in closed and confined spaces, termed as Claustrophobia, will typically try their best to avoid being put in that certain situation. Through graded/gradual exposure, therapists will try to coax them into facing their fear little by little. Initially by putting them in a large yet close area, then gradually reducing the enclosed space through each session. With this method, they are slowly facing their fear and coming to term with certain facts and realities. At the very end of the treatment, most claustrophobic people would now be able to withstand and curb their fears and are no longer fit to be called claustrophobic.

Graded/Gradual exposure is connected to CBT and may actually promote it since it also does what CBT does. It alters the way that individuals think and how they perceive certain things. With graded/gradual exposure, individuals are faced with their fears and shown what reality is actually like and different alternatives from their perspective.

Graded/gradual exposure also changes the way a person reacts, responds and behaves in a certain situation. It transforms the way they used to react since it is also connected to the way they think. Thoughts are the root of what stems from their behavior. Due to the fact that it changed their thoughts, it also ultimately made an impact on their behavioral aspect.

In CBT, an individual who has a fear of heights (acrophobia) will have to alter the way they perceive their fear. When placed in a situation that involves heights, they need to alter their negative thoughts and transform these into positive ones. Once this is done, their mind will relax along with their body and act more naturally instead of screaming in fear.

People with this fear are slowly exposed to different height ranges. As they gradually go higher while they progress, they will learn that their fear will slowly disappear. Once it disappears, their mind would have already been altered with favorable as well as positive ideas and their behavior towards the situation would have also changed from screaming or panting in anxiety to calm composure.

Activity Scheduling

This is a prominent Cognitive Behavioral therapy technique that is often regarded to be effective and efficient for individuals. This is also known to be very helpful for those who experience or deal with different psychological problems, especially depression.

People who are battling with mental disorders, such as depression, are often finding it tough to stay active and in fact, would then to lay on their bed throughout the entire day. So, in order to avoid being passive the entire time, activity scheduling is one of the many solutions they can use in order to solve their passive state and make an effort to become much more productive for the entire day.

Activity scheduling includes taking a part in different activities and behaviors that they normally wouldn't do as a result of anxiety, depression, and other psychological problems they might be currently facing. It entails a two-step process that can essentially help the individual be a lot better in the end.

Starting off, it begins with monitoring personal activities. Individuals have to take note of their activities throughout the entire week and see the different things they have achieved throughout the course of a week. This can show people that they can actually achieve a lot of things if they put their heart to it. Once the set of activities are listed and made, looking at it will improve the individual's mood when they realize the different things they were actually able to accomplish. Secondly, they would have to rate the intensity of the symptoms of depression they are experiencing alongside each activity. Through this, they can be able to identify the different activities that can actually be more helpful for them and keep their mind off of disturbing or depressive thoughts. If they look more into the pattern of activities that help them become happier and see the connection of each activity, they can devise an itinerary of things that can introduce wellness and possibly cure depression.

It is used to promote CBT since it caters to the way an individual acts in every situation. It monitors their movement and ways of behaving in a certain scenario. Through this, their behavioral aspect can be influenced and aided significantly. Activity scheduling is actually one of the many activities that can help an individual in their CBT journey.

Activity scheduling can be essential in pointing out the different activities that can promote wellness and happiness for an individual. In this process, they are given a specific tool to find out which ones are actually helping them overcome this illness and what makes it worse. Activity scheduling is often used by different therapists to treat depression from all over the world. When used effectively and accurately, it can lead to great results.

Behavioral Activation

Another Cognitive Behavioral Therapy exercise that can be used in treating several psychological disorders is Behavioral Activation. This technique enables us to get the deeper meaning and connection between a person's thoughts and behaviors. As mentioned before, thoughts and behaviors are interconnected with one another. Each aspect significantly impacts the other. Thoughts are deemed to be the root of everything. If a person has negative thoughts running through their mind, they will most likely tend to do negative acts and express negative behavior as well. These factors create a chain reaction with one another, if one aspect is touched or bothered, the other one will most likely follow in its way.

CBT is known to be extremely helpful for aiding different mental disorders. Behavioral Activation is one of the CBT skills that can ultimately help individuals overcome their psychological problems and create a better life for them in the future. Behavioral Activation is also noted by many therapists to be extremely useful in treating depression. It involves a long process that will ultimately lead to a better and fitter state of mind.

This process starts with getting to know your own feelings and coming to terms with the things you are currently experiencing. Individuals have to understand how they feel, where these emotions come from and what triggers them. Afterwards, they need to take note of the things they typically do on a daily basis. When this is done, they have to find out what they want to get out of life. They should see their goals and objectives. Then, their energy has to be directed towards wellness and motivation to do the things they want and accomplish their objectives. Ultimately, it all depends on having a good and positive change, even if it is little by little just to show progress in their activities.

For a greater understanding about behavioral activation, here's an example of how it's used. A man who deals with anxiety and depression often has different moods throughout the day/ week. There are days wherein he'd feel ecstatic and joyous and some where he feels extremely depressed. Then, when he actually takes note of the different things he has done throughout the day, he would have noticed that there are actually some activities that are considered to be emotional triggers for him. Since he is aware of the things that might potentially trigger him, he tries his best to stay away from those emotional triggers to keep a calm and collected vibe. He changes the way he acts towards these specific situations which evidently also would change his mood throughout the entire day. So, in this method he was able to identify the different emotional triggers he includes in his daily routine and was able to find a way to deal with those triggers.

Behavioral Activation is a useful and oft used tool in Cognitive Behavioral Therapy because it also deals with the cognitive and behavioral aspect. It helps a person to understand his/her situation and come to terms with their daily activities which may be impeding them from leading a good and normal life. It helps them figure out a way to negate their unfavorable thoughts and turn them into positive ones.

Problem Solving

Problem Solving is also another common and notable technique used in Cognitive Behavioral Therapy. In this method, individuals are taught on how to solve their issues, cope with the different problems they are faced with and try to regain better control over their lives. Problem solving uses a unique way in dealing with psychological problems. It directly deals with life's challenges and takes it head on. It immediately faces the problems with the use of cognitive and behavioral interventions.

This method teaches individuals how to have an active role when making decisions for an extremely difficult decision. As a result from repeated disappointments or chronic mood problems, some individuals may prefer to take the back seat and get a passive role during tough times. However, problem solving is here to teach individuals that they have to get more initiative and do whatever it takes to arrive at the goal they want.

This treatment gives one specific problem that may also apply to different situations in life wherein people can use that example problem and relate it with other real-life situations that may enable them to make better and more productive decisions all on their own. If an individual's problem solving skills are enhanced, it may lead to a surge of self confidence and other positive impacts on one's life.

When it comes to problem solving, there are actually four different core items that individuals have to take note of. The primary component of problem solving is distinguishing the problem orientation. Different people have different approaches to various problems. All these people have their own technique on how to solve a problem and how the way they think in order to address it.

So, knowing how you approach a problem, how you act towards it and the methods you take in order to solve it is very crucial in problem solving. There are some people who are much more comfortable in using the submissive approach. In this way, they can get rid of the problem immediately and not have to deal with it anymore. On the other hand, there are also different individuals who are much more strong-willed and outspoken, but do not take the problem into much consideration. They immediately jump to conclusions and speak their mind without processing all the information or thinking about the consequences. This aggressive behavior is a product of a compulsive approach.

The second item is clearly pinpointing the root cause of your problem. Misdiagnosing your own problems is quite a common thing to do. However, you must not be blinded by the things you feel but rather look at the situation clearly and see what the main factor is. As an example, you are having anxiety and stress at work. Some people might blame themselves and think it's their fault because they feel these things when, in reality, it's actually their work environment that's making them feel that way. The real problem in this equation is not their stress and anxiety, but rather the things they experience at work and the amount of tasks they have to accomplish per day.

The next core component of problem solving is brainstorming. Individuals must find different solutions and alternatives to solve their problems. After performing the two steps mentioned earlier, this step is actually the easiest yet most crucial step of all. Individuals simply have to find a positive solution to solve their negative problems. However, if they miscalculate the situation and end up doing more damage than good, then it might cause negative results in the end. Take note of as many solutions as you can and slowly eliminate each one to determine the best solution for you.

The last and most important step of all is Taking Action. All of the things you've done in the past will only go to waste if you don't take action. This step will determine the viability and effectiveness of your problem solving skills. It implements all the things you've planned out from the first step and will ultimately decide if your problem is actually solved in the end, or simply gotten worse. Taking Action is the key component in actually solving the problem and doing something to make a difference. Through this last step, you can clearly show all the things you've been trying to do and the effort you've placed into getting positive results. Every little thing you've done in the prior steps will all lead to you taking action in your life and doing something you think is right and what's best for you.

Problem Solving connects in with CBT because it manages the way a person thinks and behaves towards a situation. Through problem solving, individuals can first assess the things they are currently thinking and finding positive ones to replace the negative ideas in order to have a positive impact. After that, it manages the way we behave towards the situation since the individuals are looking for the best solution to solve the problem. A person's rash behavior is cancelled out because he/she must plan the things he/she must say and do to promote a better and positive result.

Chapter 3: CBT And Anxiety

30 Techniques on How CBT Handles Issues

Cognitive Behavioral Therapy can be useful in dealing with certain real-life situations. In fact, CBT is probably one of the most recognized treatments in the industry today. CBT handles the cognitive and behavioral aspect of a person which will essentially help change their entire outlook and treatment of life. Through this treatment, they can understand the deeper meaning of life and exactly how to tackle specific situations that require extra effort and consideration before taking action.

CBT is adaptable to many types of psychological problems. It has a wide range of specialties wherein it can be applied and made use of. This kind of treatment has treated a lot of mental disorders ranging from anxiety to depression and phobias. The techniques used in CBT are one of the key factors in making it helpful for a lot of illnesses. It can be used in treating many kinds of problems and is proven to be effective for most. CBT is identified to be one of the best and most positive treatment for patients with basic and complex mental disorders. Since this treatment touches on the cognitive aspect on an individual, it essentially causes a greater and more positive impact and follows through a change with their future emotions and behavior.

This portion shows 30 different ways how Cognitive Behavioral Techniques that can be applied to your individual life and possibly help you in achieving a better and more positive lifestyle. It shows you different types of methods on how to deal with certain situations or problems. Through CBT, you can learn different types of techniques on how to handle depression, anxiety, phobias or other mental disorders that may bother other individuals.

How CBT Handles Anxiety

Anxiety is the sense of uneasiness an individual may feel about a certain person, object, place or situation. Sometimes taking shape as fear or worry, anxiety is such a common feeling that comes and goes in everyone's lifetime.

However, there are some that develop certain kinds of anxiety disorders that can lead them to have extreme and irrational reactions or behavioral responses. Anxiety disorders are actually psychiatric problems that can make an individual feel extreme negative emotion that may lead to unfavorable circumstances.

There are six major kinds of anxiety disorders, all of which involve certain types of anxiety and different ways on how it is triggered and addressed. Cognitive-Behavioral Therapy (CBT) is actually widely regarded by many mental health professionals as the preferred psychosocial intervention for most of them.

Aside from its impressive effectiveness, it also helps the individual lead a better life even with the disorder, as it teaches them a lot of valuable skills that will help them cope with their conditions. Listed below are some of the anxiety disorders and how CBT can help individuals overcome each one.

Generalized Anxiety Disorder (GAD)

One of the most prevalent anxiety disorders around, Generalized Anxiety Disorder (GAD) is characterized by an excessive worry about almost everything in a person's life with no particular cause or reason as to why.

Individuals who have GAD tend to make a big deal out of everything. They become anxious about everything in their life — be it their financial status, work, family, friends, or health — and are constantly preoccupied with worries that something bad might happen. They expect the worst case scenario about everything and always try to look at things from a negative point of view.

With that said, it's easy to see how GAD can make it difficult for someone to live a happy and healthy life. It can come as a hindrance for their day-to-day life and become an issue with regards to their work, family, friends and any other social activities. Some of the most common symptoms of GAD include: excessive worry or tension, tiredness, inability to rest, difficulty sleeping, headaches, mood swings, difficulty in concentrating, and nausea.

Fortunately, however, CBT has worked wonders in treating all these symptoms and more. With the help of CBT, individuals suffering from GAD can change these negative thoughts into positive ones, which will ultimately change their behaviors for the better as well.

There are a number of CBT techniques that people with GAD can apply to better manage their symptoms. For example, if you have GAD and want to feel relief from all the muscle tension in your body, you can try yoga; whereas meditation can help you stop over thinking; and breathing exercises are good to practice when you start to feel yourself getting anxious again.

Yoga has been proven to help lower a person's stress, which in turn, relaxes their muscles as well. There are a number of different yoga poses and routines you can find on the internet tailored to relieving your stress and anxiety. Some examples include: the eagle pose, the headstand, child's pose, half moon pose, and the legs up the wall pose.

If you need help getting started with how to use yoga to ease some of the distress you may feel from GAD, here is a quick rundown of how you can do it:

- Go to the gym and sign up for their yoga class.
- Or if you prefer, you can stay at home and do yoga by yourself.

- It's often best to do yoga in the afternoon or at the end of the day, as a way to decompress.
- Set up your mat, and if you want, play some relaxing music.
- Breathe in and out, deeply.
- Be aware of your breathing as you move through each pose.
- Take your time going through all the movements.
- Most importantly, enjoy yourself and keep your mind clear.

On the other hand, if the most problematic symptom of your GAD is overthinking and emotional turmoil, not muscle tension and chronic pain, then meditation just might be the CBT technique for you. Here's how you can do it:

- Download some guided meditation videos online (there's plenty on YouTube).
- Listen to them on a regular basis, preferably everyday (as you wake up or before you go to sleep is the most ideal).
- Find a quiet place to do this, where you can be alone and away from distractions.
- Devote all your attention to these 10-30 minute mediations and do not think or worry about anything else while you're doing so.

- Make it a rule that once you start meditating, you need to forget about everything else going on in your life and just focus on the present moment.
- Repeat everything the instructor is saying in the guided meditations

By meditating, you are giving your anxiety a healthy and positive outlet and releasing your physical tension from your body. The more you do it, the more peace of mind you will feel, and the easier it will be for you to overcome your anxiety.

When using CBT, a person with GAD will have a much more favorable perspective in life. Instead of always worrying and thinking about the worst case scenario, CBT reinforces an optimistic and reasonable outlook on life, which will then have a positive impact on their behavior as well. Most of the time, they'll change from a tense and edgy person to a relaxed and easygoing one that doesn't assume the worst out of everything.

Social Anxiety

Another common type of anxiety is social anxiety, characterized by an immediate distress whenever you meet or interact with unfamiliar people. Affecting over 15 million different American adults, this can be considered to be one of the most prominent types of anxiety that in the country.

Also known as "social phobia", those with social anxiety often display visible signs or symptoms that indicate their discomfort towards the situation. Some of those symptoms may include blushing, stuttering, increased heart rate, sweating, being awkward or boring, and, worst case scenario, experiencing a full-blown anxiety attack.

If you are one of the many people suffering from social anxiety, than you'd understand how much of a disturbance it can be in your life. Because it hinders you from a lot of social interactions, you may have a hard time in connecting with other people and making new friends. This may also affect your personality, as it can keep you from enjoying yourself when you're out with friends since you don't really have the courage to stand up and talk for yourself. You fear becoming involved in social situations and you try your best to keep to yourself as much as possible and avoid interacting with other people at all costs.

Although individuals with social anxiety know that their reaction to the situation may be over-the-top or unreasonable, they just can't seem to keep the anxiety and emotions at bay. They often seem powerless when battling this emotion and sometimes, in the end, anxiety takes over their lives. Due to these symptoms, they may try their best to avoid situations where they might get pressured into socializing with other people at all costs.

In order to overcome social anxiety, many individuals have turned to therapy. Cognitive Behavioral Therapy (CBT) is one of the most common and used treatment for this certain problem. With an array of different methods and techniques, CBT can help you overcome your social anxiety by getting to the heart of the problem: your thoughts.

Everything we feel and do stems from our thoughts. So, CBT alters the way individuals process information and turns negative thoughts into positive ones. In turn, it generates positive moods that may also lead to favorable actions or behavior. When relating CBT to social anxiety, it tries to get rid of all the negative thoughts that may pop up into your mind when you're about to interact with other people.

For example, when you're meeting new people, you might instantly think that they might hate you or dislike the way you talk or act immediately. However, with CBT, it eliminates this type of thinking and keeps an open and positive mindset of the things that may happen. CBT can also help individuals calm themselves down when experiencing a panic attack or when having an inner conflict colored with anxiety.

There are some CBT techniques that are specially designed to help individuals overcome different types of situations. For example, Cognitive Restructuring can be used in treating social phobia. It can be crucial in understanding your triggers, controlling your mood swings and keeping a positive mindset on everything.

Typically, individuals would have to go to therapists for their own CBT treatment. However, there are some ways that it can still help you when you're on your own. You simply have to follow a series of steps in order to overcome the situation.

- Make an effort to calm yourself down before you interact with someone else.
- Look at the current situation you're faced with. Describe it to yourself.
- Assess how that particular situation made you feel and identify those feelings.
- Go through your thoughts about that certain scenario and scan through what your mind immediately thought of when you faced that situation. The first few thoughts that pop into your head are your "automatic thoughts."
- Narrow in on your negative automatic thoughts. Ask yourself what triggered these thoughts.
- Now, are these triggers reasonable? Is it your negative view of yourself or the situation justifiable? Be as objective as you can and try not to let your emotions get in the way.

- Soon, you will realize that your thoughts are only misguided and aren't actually true at all. They're just the lies you sometimes tell yourself which feed your insecurity.
- Work on erasing these thoughts from your mind by replacing them with the truth. For example, whenever you think, "Nobody likes me," automatically reply with "Hey! That's just not true! [This certain person] likes me!"

Cognitive restructuring can be extremely helpful for those individuals who are trying to control or assess the way they react to certain scenarios. It can help them lighten their mood.

As for those individuals who still need to calm their nerves whenever they are faced with a situation they dread so much, they can also try relaxation techniques. While we've already talked a lot about yoga, meditation, and breathing exercises to help you relax, here is another technique you can use to calm yourself down:

- Take a seat and sit with your back straight.
- Place one hand along your chest and the other one on your stomach .
- Inhale through your nose. You will notice your hand on your stomach area moves more while your other hand should only move slightly.

- Breathe out with your mouth. This will cause your stomach to move in while your chest will still move slightly.
- Repeat this process and count each deep breath you take. Imagine that with every exhale, you are releasing negative energy from your body.
- After a while, your muscle tension will decrease and you will feel a lot calmer than you were beforehand. Keep doing this until you no longer feel any distress or anxiety.

Panic Disorder

Panic attacks are characterized by out-of-the-blue emotions or feelings of trepidation when, in fact, there is no real reason to be afraid. Having recurrent panic attacks for seemingly no reason at all is what is known as a panic disorder. This is mostly found in young adults aged 20 and above. However, it can also be experienced by other children who also have panic-like symptoms.

Anxiety disorders can greatly affect a person's life. Always being at risk of spontaneous panic attacks may lead them to avoid going out, and thus, isolate themselves from others. Individuals with panic disorder typically live their lives in fear of getting another panic attack, so they try their best to control it or maybe even hide from other people.

Individuals with panic disorder often spend most of their time fearing the possibility of having another panic attack (a fear known as "agoraphobia"). Agoraphobia is when individuals stay on high-alert for potential panic attacks and always keep their guard up in case real danger arrives. This can cause them to avoid certain places like shopping malls, festivals, movie theaters, grocery stores, and the like.

With different types of indications, panic disorder typically includes symptoms like sweating, rapid heart rate, chills, trembling, or always sensing potential danger in every situation. In order to control symptoms like these, there are a lot of different treatments created for panic disorder. Cognitive Behavioral Therapy is also commonly used by therapists in treating patients with a wide variety of mental problems, including panic disorder.

As explained in previous chapters, CBT deals with a person's thought patterns, emotions, and behaviors. It deals with the cognitive and behavioral factors of psychological problems and seeks to transform a person's negative ideas and behaviors into more positive ones. When dealing with panic disorder, it is important for CBT to eliminate their constant fear of being in danger and replace them with the assurance that not all situations will lead to an untimely death.

There are several CBT techniques that can help individuals with panic disorder overcome their condition or calm themselves whenever a panic attack arises. Developing your calming skills is one of the most notable techniques. If you're struggling with panic disorder, try this basic guide on how to ease your mind and prevent a panic attack from escalating once you sense anxiety knocking on your mind's door.

- Take long, deep breaths.
- Are you anxious? Be honest with yourself about what you feel and identify your emotions.
- Work towards accepting these feelings, even the negative ones like fear.
- Once you've accomplished this, remind yourself that your thoughts only have power over you if you let them. Your feelings do not control you, but rather, you control them.
- Assess your thoughts and ask yourself if these are actually realistic or reasonable (much like what you did before, in dealing with social anxiety).
- Visualize a calming scenario and go to your happy place. This can be a pristine, white sand beach with the cool sea breeze in your face; or a lush, green mountain top overlooking a beautiful sunset. Wherever it is, go to it.
- Repeat a positive, self-affirming mantra in your mind. Examples include:

This is only a trick played by my brain; I am more powerful than these negative thoughts.
I am strong and powerful and I will not surrender.
I am getting stronger and healthier.
I can do this. I believe in myself.
No matter how terrible this feeling may be, it will pass. And I'll be okay again.

- Focus on the things on hand and the positive side of everything.

Obsessive Compulsive Disorder

Obsessive Compulsive Disorder, also known as OCD, is a psychological problem that involves uncontrollable ideas or thought patterns and behaviors that you feel obliged or the sudden urge to do. These are unwanted thoughts, obsessions or images that enter the individual's mind may serve as a great discomfort that will essentially turn into a hindrance between the individual's daily activities and their mindset. Afterwards, the individual will have no choice but to participate or perform repetitive acts and behaviors in order to control or deal with these thoughts.

OCD can greatly affect one's lifestyle. With these thoughts and compulsions, they will stop their day-to-day activities and try to engage or handle their thoughts. This type of mental problem can begin as early as the age of 7 and progress later on. Typically affecting male children over female ones, the rate of people with OCD will increase more on the women's side in the long run. There are different types of obsessions and compulsion when it comes to OCD.

For example, people who get easily worked up over getting in contact with dirt or germs often have this idea that it may get them sick; a type of OCD known as "contamination obsession." Other times, OCD can take the form of a need for symmetry in all things, which can lead individuals to arranging everything in a specific way and organizing everything because of an irrational belief like, "If this is not arranged by size, something bad will surely happen".

It can cause a great impact on their school, work, social and personal life. This can let them have a hard time getting to sleep, maintaining hygiene, forming friendships, uphold their grades or participating in any type of social or athletic performances.
There are different types of symptoms when it comes to OCD. Cognitive symptoms include constantly thinking "I am responsible for everything", "What if I'll get sick because of this?" and "I must know everything!"

There are also physical symptoms that may be identified, such as muscle tension, constant pain in the stomach, dizziness, headaches and feeling detached from your own body. For further implication that an individual has this type of psychological problem, there are also emotional symptoms that you can also check for, like anxiety, sadness, guilt, shame, and anger.

CBT is one of best and most recommended ways to treat OCD. Since it focuses on the cognitive and behavioral aspect of a person, it can be perfect to treat a disorder like OCD.

CBT tries to replace their unwanted thoughts and images with positive ones and gain a much more positive outlook in life. After working on the cognitive aspect, positive thoughts will then lead to positive emotions that will likely produce better behaviors towards situations. This can allow them to control the way they react to certain scenarios and handle their compulsion.

There are also some helpful CBT techniques that individuals may use whenever they feel those unwanted images creeping at their doorstep again or if they become unsettled by the emotions they're having. One of those techniques is by finding the root cause of your thoughts and emotions. This can be done by:

- Take a moment to stop and assess everything that is currently happening in this moment.
- Question the OCD and what it needs you to feel (e.g. be in control of everything or trying to make you feel safe).
- Come up with at least 3 other methods you can do to make you feel that way without paying attention to the OCD.
- If you can't, then write down what it is you're worrying about and set a time for you to worry about

it later (for example, after you've finished your homework or project).

- Then, when you come back to it, you'll find that most of the time, you've lost interest in wasting your time and worrying about what it is your OCD bothered you with before, and you can go about the rest of your day in peace.

Another helpful technique is doing progressive muscle relaxation or PMR. This can be partnered with different deep breathing exercises to help release all the tension that builds up within your muscle and help you get to a calm and relaxing manner. This can battle OCD since it makes you feel uncomfortable whenever you feel the urge to do something. With PMR, you can relinquish those thoughts and feel relaxed at the same time. PMR starts with a process like:

- Sit in a quiet and comfortable room.
- Remove all unnecessary and tight clothing or items that may cause any uneasiness.
- Sit in a comfortable position.
- Take some slow, deep and even breaths.
- Pay attention to all your muscles starting with your face. Clench your muscles as you inhale and release the tension along your face muscles when you exhale while practicing your breathing technique.

- Repeat twice before proceeding to other areas like shoulders, arms, stomach, butt, legs, feet and repeat the process for each of them.

These techniques may just help individuals with OCD handle the tension in their body and fight off the unwanted images. However, professional help is also important. With long CBT sessions with your own therapist, you can overcome this problem and possibly live a better life.

Post-Traumatic Stress Disorder

Post-Traumatic Stress Disorder (PTSD) is a type of anxiety disorder that stems from traumatic, stressful or frightening events that may lead an individual to experience traumatic episodes that force them to relive that very same event.

PTSD is known to have a major effect on people's lives. This can impede them from trying certain things, going to different places, or socializing with other people normally. A traumatizing event (such as a car accident or a natural calamity) can lead individuals to constantly think of that occasion and experience horrific flashbacks, as well as nightmares. People with PTSD tend to avoid things that remind them of that experience. So, each time they see a trigger they experience panic attacks or flashbacks. This can restrain them from experiencing other things and will eventually isolate them from others.

This type of anxiety disorder should be treated as early as possibly to ease their psychological distress immediately and avoid any damaging, long-term effects. Symptoms of PTSD include recurring flashbacks of a certain traumatic experience, constant nightmares about it, and getting terrifying and negative thoughts relating to it. Along with this, people with PTSD also experience accelerated heart rates, profuse sweating, anxiousness, and at times, emotional numbness.

One of the top treatments recommended by therapists is Cognitive Behavioral Therapy. CBT helps individuals overcome the trauma and eliminate negative thoughts about that scenario and replace them with positive ones that can help them sleep better at night. It can also change the manner they react to a certain object, situation or person that might trigger their PTSD. Trauma-focused CBT can use a variety of techniques that will help individuals triumph over this mental disorder and find other healthier and more positive outlets to direct their energy towards.

There are some helpful CBT techniques that can aid those struggling with PTSD. Mindfulness meditation is one of the best CBT techniques in treating this particular anxiety disorder, as it allows individuals to calm their minds while also focusing on the present factors around them. This can be done by following these steps:

- Sit up straight on a chair or sit cross-legged on the floor.
- Take deep breaths, in and out. Pay attention to everything that happens to your body in this moment.
- Notice the way your body feels as you inhale and exhale. Focus all your attention on these bodily sensations.
- Afterwards, begin to redirect your attention on what's happening around you, like the sounds outside or the thoughts running through your mind.
- Take note and accept each idea without assessing if it's positive or negative.
- Whenever you find yourself judging them, return your focus on your breathing and start the process again.

This teaches a person to keep a calm and level head while reflecting on their thoughts and understanding what's going on inside them. For those afflicted with PTSD, it's important to stay focused on the present rather than the past, which is why mindfulness meditation is such an apt treatment for them.

It is important to come to terms with the things that happened to you in the past. However, it is not okay to allow it to ruin your future and all the good things that may still happen in your life by staying stuck there. PTSD is a serious condition, and only when you learn and accept the fact that you have to keep moving forward in life, can you truly heal from it. CBT can help you do this.

Chapter 4: CBT And Depression

How to Use CBT for Depression

The term depression has been thrown around so lightly in today's culture that it has now come to mean any feeling of sadness or lethargy. However, depression is much more serious with that, as those who struggle with it already know.

Called the "common cold of mental illnesses" because of how prevalent it is, depression greatly affects an individual's thoughts, emotions and behaviors in a negative manner. Living with depression is like coasting through life, feeling unmotivated to do anything and drowning in self-loathing. Most people who are depressed struggle to even get out of bed in the morning, much less do anything productive with their day. There are over six major kinds of depression, each with different factors causing its arrival.

There are a lot of ways on how to tackle depression. An individual can opt to undergo different types of therapy in order to take their mind off matters and try to heal. Depression is an extremely difficult and complex topic to touch on. With a variety of options to choose from on how to handle this type of psychological problem, one of the most prominent and effective methods used by multiple individuals and therapist all over the world is psychotherapy.

There are different types of psychotherapy but the most used and found to be most helpful for patients is Cognitive Behavioral Therapy (CBT). This particular form of therapy was specially designed to treat depression (as you might recall from reading the "History of CBT" segment in Chapter 1).

Handling the thought pattern, emotions and behavioral aspect of a person, it can allow them to get something greater in life and not dwell on the negative side of everything. CBT is a wide and complex treatment that is known to be helpful in treating a variety of mental illnesses, depression being one of them.

Listed below are some ways on how each individual can make use of Cognitive Behavioral Therapy when faced with different kinds of depression.

Major Depression

Major Depression is one of the most common types of depression. There are approximately 16.2 million adults suffering from it in the US alone. Also termed as "Major Depressive Disorder", "Unipolar Depression", or "Classic Depression", this kind of depression is characterized by feeling too much grief or gloom, being overly fatigued most of the time, having a hard time sleeping well at night, losing interest in activities that once excite you, not wanting to eat as much as you did before, feeling hopeless or experiencing anxiety, and perhaps contemplating about self-harm or suicide.

However, this type of depression does not typically stem from a person's surrounding or situation. A person could have everything one may dream of and still have depression. Major Depression can last for as long as week or possibly throughout one's entire lifetime. Causing a hindrance between their social and personal life, major depression can keep you from enjoying everything you love about life and isolate yourself from others. Negative thinking patterns may lead you to an unhealthy lifestyle. So how do you overcome it?

Cognitive Behavioral Therapy is one of the most common and effective methods used by therapists to help their clients overcome their depression. Enabling the individual to alter their thought patterns, Cognitive Behavioral Therapy (CBT) faces the problem head on and acknowledges the situation. This does not make any excuses or hide you from the truth, but rather allows you to accept the situation and think of a silver lining for it.

A lot of its success comes from the fact that CBT touches on the most important aspects of a person's life, which are their thoughts, emotions, and behaviors. CBT helps you eliminate your negative thoughts and replace them with more positive ones. As it alters negative thoughts into positive ones, it also impacts the emotions and behavior positively like a domino effect. It also deals with dysfunctional behaviors and changing them for the better.

There are some specific CBT techniques that can help individuals deal with major depression, but most experts would agree that the most suitable technique to apply here would be cognitive restructuring.

Depressed individuals tend to have negative automatic thoughts. Through cognitive restructuring, they can deal with this and replace it with more positive ones that can help them function better, mentally and emotionally. Here's a guide on how to use cognitive restructuring on your own:

- Assess the situation. Find the negative aspect that's upsetting you
- Keep track of your negative emotions. Describe them in your journal and rate the intensity of each emotion.
- Pay attention to all the things you automatically think of whenever you encounter a difficult situation and keep track of how much you believe in each of them
- Examine these thoughts and see if they are realistic or not
- Generate better and positive thoughts that are realistic and seems more likely to happen when compared to your automatic thoughts.
- Evaluate the process and repeat as much as necessary.

These techniques can be extremely helpful in dealing with a depressive episode on your own. However, it is important to remember that professional help can sometimes be the better option, especially when dealing with depression which can often leave the person feeling unmotivated at all to complete their therapy and hopeless about ever recovering from their mental illness.

Major Depression can be treated with CBT in different healthcare clinics. Individuals have to assess their own state of mind and once things becomes too hard for them to handle, they should talk to other people, like therapists, about their problems. This way, they can live a better life and slowly regain control.

Persistent Depression

Also known as "dysthymia" or "chronic depression", persistent depression is the most recurrent of all types of depression, typically manifesting in episodes that last as long as 2 years and return throughout an individual's lifetime.

It may not come as powerful as Major Depression but it may still take its own toll on the one that may be experiencing it. The feeling of being sad and hopeless, having second thoughts about yourself, lack of interest, and problem of being happy during joyous occasions may be a sign of this type of depression.

It can also change your perspective on how life works. Symptoms may fade out for a while before coming back as clear and powerful as ever, making it difficult for a person to feel like they have any semblance of control over their lives.

Therapy is one of the many ways in overcoming this particular type of depression. Cognitive Behavioral Therapy (CBT) can be essential in dealing with a long-term depression such as persistent depression. This kind of depression may be an occasional experience for some individuals. There are moments when they seem to be normal and happy, and other times wherein they just can't seem to see the bright side to anything. When dark moments come, it is important to use CBT in handling this situation.

CBT replaces negative thoughts with positive ones and changes the way one may behave around this kind of situation. It can possibly alter your trail of thought and behavior in order for you to see the better things in life. When people with persistent depression make use of CBT, it can be possible for them to get over this long-term illness and go on with their own life happily.

A common CBT technique that can help you get through persistent depression on your own is problem analysis. Also known as "situational analysis", it helps people see the problem objectively and find a positive solution for it. Problem analysis starts with:

- Finding the problem
- Understanding the problem and how it works
- Dividing the situation into smaller parts in order to understand it better
- Finding out what your goal is and what you want to work towards

- Finding positive ways to reach your goal and move on from the problem

Problem analysis can be helpful in treating persistent depression since it can help them overcome the problem in a positive manner. This CBT technique will aid them in triumphing over depression and help them on their way to recovery. It also teaches them how to respond to specific situations that may be complex to handle.

Manic Depression

Another term for Manic Depression is "Bipolar Disorder". This is composed of different periods called Mania and Hypomania. An individual's moods can be replaced between a state of feeling extreme euphoria and extreme depression. There are different moods for different periods, changing without any sensible reason.

Mania is a severe period that may last for around 7 days which is then followed by Hypomania, a less powerful experience that may still cause an impact onto an individual. There are different symptoms existing to distinguish this illness, most of which are similar to major depression. However, indications of the manic phase may be increased self-confidence, destructive behavior, high energy, less sleep, and a euphoric state.

When tackling something as complex as Manic Depression, CBT can do a great job in handling this illness. Directly impacting one's behavior, Bipolar Disorder can severely impact one's way of life and alter their actions and thought pattern. So, CBT can be a great method to undertake in order to manage one's behavior and positively impact their thoughts to induce better moods and feelings for an individual.

People with Manic Depression can overcome this illness through intensive CBT sessions and talking with other people in order to calm and control their mood swings. This can help them become better and gain better control over their life again. There are a variety of CBT techniques that individuals with bipolar disorder can make use of. One of the most helpful ways in dealing with this particular type of depression is by controlling your cognitive distortions, which you can do by making sure you are not:

- Overgeneralizing - jumping to conclusions because of a single instance (i.e., you miss the shot once and immediately think that you're a bad player and you can't play any sport well)
- Thinking All-or-Nothing – seeing the world in terms of absolutes, meaning people or circumstances are either all good or all bad
- Taking Things Too Personally – believing that everything bad that happens is because of you (i.e. "The teacher was mad at the class because I forgot my homework.")
- Minimizing the Positive – discounting the good things that happen because you believe they are by luck or something out of your control

- Maximizing the Negative – dwelling on your own failures and frustrations so much that they keep you from being happy

This can kind of cognitive reconstruction can help individuals with manic depression to overcome their depressive episodes as well as controlling their emotions. The process allows individuals to take control of their cognitive process and change their behavior. So, individuals with this type of depression can use this process whenever they feel the need to assess their thoughts and behaviors.

Perinatal Depression

Perinatal Depression is a depressive disorder known to be experienced by pregnant women during or after their pregnancy. Also called as postpartum depression, hormones produced during pregnancy can generate different mood swings and unusual behavior. This feeling can also be increased because of the difficulties a mother must go through after giving birth, such as lack of sleep and constant care of their newborn child. Symptoms that accompany this illness is the feeling of sadness, regular anxiety, worry regarding your baby's health, difficulty in caring for yourself or your baby, and possibly harming one's self or the baby.

Postpartum depression is extremely risky and dangerous when left untreated. This particular illness can possibly endanger the mother and child's health and well-being.

When dealing with Perinatal Depression, CBT can help mothers see a better outlook on life with new circumstances. This therapy can allow them to deal with their negative and unfavorable thoughts about their new life and replace them with positive ones that will allow them to see the bright side of things. Cognitive Behavioral Therapy will also allow them to adjust and change their behavior that may positively impact the situation they are currently in.

Through CBT, new mothers can see different methods on how to handle their every life and find out better options on how to address various situations favorably. CBT can help these women deal with the way they feel and the way they handle things. CBT is a wide and complex process which involves a lot of different procedures before actually arriving at the conclusion. With this notion, there are actually a lot of different CBT techniques that can help these individuals deal with their thoughts and behaviors better. One notable CBT process that is sure to assist mothers with perinatal depression is the Thought Challenge Exercise. The process starts with this:

- Look at the situation objectively
- Identify the feelings you possess regarding the situation and recognize them
- Challenge your thought patterns and the way you behave by seeing the evidences

- Alter these negative and unfavorable thoughts, emotions and behaviors into better ones by identifying them and looking for better solutions to handle things

Through this process, they can learn how to deal with things better and in a much more positive and realistic manner. This may allow them to avoid any type of potential danger within themselves for their own safety and for the baby. Although this can help them go through different situations on their own, it is still important to get everything treated by a therapist with the proper CBT procedure.

Atypical Depression

This kind of depression is not a long-term depression. It is actually a subtype of another type of depression, which is Major Depression. However, it regularly comes back whenever life seems to be getting down. Atypical depression goes away whenever good things happen and comes back when they don't. Don't let the name confuse you, the term "Atypical" does not signify its rareness. It actually means it has different symptoms and signs when compared to other types of depression.

This can be challenging to address, considering that you might also seem baffled whether or not you're actually experiencing it. Symptoms that lead to Atypical Depression are increased appetite, insomnia, sleeping for more hours than usual, heaviness in your body, and sensitivity to comments and rejection.

The usage of CBT can be essential in battling this illness. In atypical depression, CBT can be used whenever these phases come back. Through this, individuals can positively change their train of thought and possibly replace negative ideas with better ones. This can give them a positive outlook in life and may allow them to be a better person.

There are various CBT techniques to help individuals go through this depression when they're on their own. A common one is by exercising. It is known to relax muscles, take your mind off of current matters (or from traumatic events), and maybe even allow the individual to practice staying relaxed and calm. There are some types that may help people with atypical depression in exercising to handle their depression. These are:

- Find a specific workout that you actually like
- Identify a specific workout goal that you would like to accomplish (something that is easy and attainable)
- Find exercises that also offers social support
- Make it part of your daily itinerary
- Find something that can be convenient to do
- Even if you feel depressed or out of the mood, do it anyway

In this method, they can also change their behavior towards different situation and learn to act better. When seeking help from professionals, CBT can be very effective. Talking to others about an illness is always brave, but trying to fix it is even braver.

Situational Depression

Situational Depression may often look like Major Depression, however it is triggered by certain scenarios or situations in life. It is known to be as an adjustment disorder with depressed mood. It may be induced by situations like death of a loved one, a life-threatening event, abusive relationships, or financial issues. These situations may bring about situational depression along with its symptoms such as frequent crying, sadness, anxiety, social withdrawal and over-fatigue.

Situational Depression is becoming depressed over a particular event or scenario that happened, or is happening, in one's life. Through CBT, individuals may see a better way to cope with their situation and focus on a better and more favorable thought pattern. They may change the way they think about life onto a much more positive way and control the way they behave towards the situation.

This type of depression can be extremely hard to handle. When left without treatment, it may also progress into different types of complex and serious mental illnesses that will greatly impact one's lifestyle. There are various CBT techniques to choose from, in order to handle this problem. However, Journaling is known to be quite helpful and calming to do. It lets individuals assess their thoughts, improve their behavior and mood, and also attain a relaxed and calm feature that will essentially help them in the future. Effectively journaling your thoughts for depression can be done by:

- Changing your viewpoint to avoid any biases and to look at the situation objectively
- Writing down all your emotions and the way you feel about the situation
- Incorporating it into your everyday routine
- Attempt new things
- Stay focused on the positive side and ignore the negative side
- Jot down all the potential triggers for you
- List positive items on a daily basis

CBT can help these individuals achieve a better perspective in life. Simply by assessing your own self and talking to others when you have a chance can give a great impact to you. Talking about your own illness can help you rather than shame you. It is never wrong to be fighting battles of the mind.

Chapter 5: CBT For Fears And Phobias

How To Use CBT For Fears and Phobias

Fear is a natural biological response in humans. In fact, according to evolution, it is largely due to fear that human beings survived throughout the years and evolved to adapt better to their environments. Fear has become essential in our progress as a species and in our day-to-day survival, even when we are no longer fighting with wild beasts to survive.

With that said, while it's normal to feel fear towards certain objects or situations, sometimes this fear can get out of hand and become a phobia. Phobias are an exaggerated and recurrent fear response that's characterized by an active avoidance of a certain object, activity or situation. It typically develops during the formative years and persists into adulthood.

Often times, the person suffering from phobia knows that his/her fear is irrational and not proportional to the actual threat posed by the stimulus. This reasoning, however, doesn't do much to help them overcome their phobias. In some cases, the phobia isn't severe enough to require treatment, especially if the feared stimulus can easily be avoided. However, there are also others who do not have this luxury and may find their personal functioning and well-being impaired by their phobias.

With that said, a lot of people seeking professional help are looking to treat their phobias. Fortunately for them, the prognosis is generally good and success rates are high. Among the most common clinical treatments for phobias are: antidepressants, anxiolytics, beta-blockers, psychodynamic therapy, behavioral therapy, and of course, at the very forefront of this endeavor is cognitive-behavioral therapy (CBT). Through CBT, individuals can better manage, minimize, and sometimes even eliminate their fears and phobias altogether.

It's easy to understand why CBT would be the most ideal treatment method for fears and phobias. More often than not, specific phobias are deeply rooted in an individual's dysfunctional beliefs, which in turn influence their maladaptive behaviors regarding a certain stimulus. That's why CBT works best, because it focuses a lot on redirecting and controlling this problematic thinking and changing it to result in more functional behavioral responses.

If you're afflicted with a specific phobia and want to be free of your irrational fears, then CBT can definitely help you. So let's discuss the most common kinds of specific phobias and break down how to treat each and every one of them with CBT.

Arachnophobia

Starting off the list, the number one most common kind of specific phobia is arachnophobia (the fear of spiders and arachnids), which affects over 30.5% of the general US population or 1 in every 3 women and 1 in every 4 men.

Now, it's understandable why many of us would be afraid of spiders and scorpions, because of their unsettling appearance and venomous bites and stings. However, arachnophobic individuals experience a more intense fear than most, as merely the sight or image of a spider is enough to paralyze them with terror. So much so that it might keep them from being able to work properly, study well, sleep, or enjoy social activities.

What's more is, arachnophobia is quite unreasonable because only a minority of arachnid species is actually dangerous to humans, and most of them inhabit the wilderness or the desert. Yet, someone with arachnophobia will still search every room they enter to check if there are any spiders or scorpions. If they do find one, they will most likely keep a close watch on it the entire time and feel tense in its presence even if it's just a harmless domestic spider.

The CBT technique of choice in resolving arachnophobia (and all the other specific phobias mentioned on this list, you'll find) is exposure and desensitization therapy. Exposure and desensitization therapy, as I've explained before in the previous chapters, involves the systematic exposure of the individual to their object of fear until he/she eventually learns to feel less anxious about it and cope with their distress in a more functional way.

While I've already discussed the basics of how to conduct exposure therapy on yourself, I'll run through them again and contextualize it to this specific phobia.

- If you are afflicted with arachnophobia, work through your fear little by little in a series of gradual exposure exercises.
- At first, you might want to try simply thinking about a spider,
- When you do, resist your usual fear response (i.e., screaming, crying, tensing up).
- If this is hard for you to do, try meditating or repeating a positive mantra (i.e., "I am safe, I am okay, it's just a thought.")
- Try to do this for at least 5 minutes.
- Then, try it again the next day, but this time for 10 minutes.
- Repeat the process until you feel comfortable enough to move on to looking at a picture of a spider.
- Once you've conquered that, try using VR technology to simulate a spider.
- Finally, be in the same room as a spider without feeling any fear or dread.

Now, the key to all of these exercises is that you learn to recondition your mind to stop fearing the spider. Avoid cringing, crying, screaming, or running away when exposed to it, and instead, talk yourself through it. Challenge your fear and rationalize it until you've truly convinced yourself that there's nothing to fear.

Acrophobia

An intense fear of heights, otherwise known as "acrophobia", can be very disruptive in a person's life as most of us often face heights every day. Whether it's going to work in a high-rise building, looking out on our apartment window, or simply riding a train over a tall bridge, it can be difficult to avoid and terrifying to endure.

Luckily, many people suffering from acrophobia report that Cognitive-Behavioral Therapy (CBT) was able to effectively help them manage, and in some cases even eliminate, their specific phobia.

CBT is effective because it confronts a person's deep-seated fears and changes their way of thinking about heights. In controlling the anxiety-inducing thought patterns of an acrophobic individual and replacing them with more positive ones, CBT is able to effectively change the behavioral responses that follow.

- What you need to do first is relax your mind. Listen to some calming music or meditate and clear your head.

- Once you're in a good headspace, begin to imagine that you are somewhere high, like a mountain top overlooking a beautiful view.

- It's crucial that you do not allow yourself to feel anxious or afraid while you do this. If you do, focus on the music, calm yourself down, and talk yourself through it.

- It helps to have a mantra, so try saying, "I am calm and safe. It's okay for me to be around heights. I feel only peace of mind."

- Then, when you feel secure enough to allow yourself to imagine being somewhere high up, try to apply it in real life as well.

- Cross a bridge or ride an elevator going up and just enjoy the view. Stay calm and act as if you don't feel any fear at all.

- If you feel panicked, take deep breaths and close your eyes.

- Relax all the muscles in your body and try to focus on a single object, like your shoes and how your feet feel in them. Or better yet, imagine that you are in your happy place until you calm down.

If you keep doing this, over time you will recondition your brain to feel no fear at all towards heights, and thus, eliminate your acrophobia.

Aerophobia is so common that, chances are, you probably suffer from it or know someone who does. This extreme fear of flying often keeps people from travelling and riding planes, which can cause them to miss out on a lot of amazing vacations and even career opportunities like attending international conferences and important meetings with foreign clients.

With that said, if you are one of the millions of people suffering from aerophobia, there's an effective solution to your problems: Cognitive-Behavioral Therapy (CBT).

Treating aerophobia with CBT is all about unlearning your maladaptive responses to heights, and in doing so, lessening your fears. Commonly, exposure and desensitization therapy is the technique of choice here, but since I've already talked about it so much, I'll teach you something else.

This technique is called "Socratic Questioning." Socratic questioning aims to help you determine how accurate and helpful your fears really are by exploring your thoughts and beliefs about them. Here is an example of how to apply this technique to treating your aerophobia.

- Start by proclaiming what you feel or believe ("I am afraid of flying and being in planes").
- Then, challenge that belief ("But why?") and answer as truthfully as you can.
- Never settle for "Just because," or "I don't know", but rather, really get to the heart of your problem ("Because I worry that it might crash. and the turbulence makes me uncomfortable").
- Explore the roots of your fears ("Why am I so afraid? I've never even been on a plane before.").
- Then, rationalize them ("Statistically speaking, the odds of being in a plane crash is 1 in 11 million" and "My friends and family fly all the time, and nothing bad ever happens to them.").

Socratic questioning helps you analyze and process a particular train of thought. With specific phobias, oftentimes there is actually no justifiable reason for them. Once you understand that there's really nothing to be afraid of, it will be easier for you to ride planes and fly, and the more you do it, the less frightened or nervous you'll feel.

Cynophobia

Next on the list is cynophobia, which refers to a severe fear of dogs. This one is particularly difficult to leave untreated, as dogs are generally seen as beloved pets. No doubt, you probably know more than a few people who have pet dogs. While it's normal to be a little bit afraid of dogs as a child, it's not normal to allow this fear to haunt you for the rest of your life and keep you from functioning well in your day-to-day life.

Someone with cynophobia is apprehensive or anxious about unfamiliar dogs, and in extreme cases, even familiar ones like a long-time family pet. This specific phobia makes it hard for them to even walk down a street without being afraid, because they worry that there might be dogs living in that certain neighborhood (and chances are, they're probably right, which only makes things worse).

Many believe that most cases of cynophobia develop from a traumatic early experience of being bitten or chased by a dog, a recent study revealed that majority of those with cynophobia have never even had any direct encounters with a dog at all. But if that's true, then how come people with this specific phobia find it so hard to overcome their fears?

Most experts believe that the answer lies in their negative thinking and misconceptions regarding dogs and the actual danger they pose, which is why CBT is their most recommended form of psychotherapy.

Similar to arachnophobia, cynophobia is also commonly treated with exposure and desensitization therapy. In fact, it applies the very same structure of the arachnophobia treatment we've discussed earlier.

- Start by thinking about dogs without fear.
- Don't move on to the next step unless you can overcome your fear of simply thinking about dogs.
- Next, imagine a dog — it's paws, it's bark, it's fur — without feeling afraid or uncomfortable.
- Then, look at pictures of dogs and remain calm.
- Try doing this with a friend, and then modeling their behavior. Most likely, they will say something along the lines of, "Awww! What a cute dog!"
- When you're ready, go to a pet shop and look at their dogs.
- The final step to overcoming your cynophobia is by petting or at least going near the dog without feeling afraid.

It also helps to learn better coping skills so that if you ever do feel afraid when doing exposure therapy, you'll know how to stop. Try to apply relaxation techniques like mindfulness meditation or progressive muscle relaxation (like what I've discussed earlier, when dealing with anxiety). Both have been proven to reduce anxiety and increase feelings of emotional well-being.

Astraphobia

Another common phobia is astraphobia, or the fear of thunder and lightning. As you might imagine, this can be a stressful affliction to have, especially in times of stormy weather. Sometimes even a darkening sky or light rain is enough to cause someone with astraphobia to start sweating, shaking, breathing heavily, and have their heart racing. Can you imagine being on the verge of a panic attack every time a bit of rain starts to fall down? It would make life very unpleasant, indeed.

Those with astraphobia often become obsessed with the weather and waste a lot of their time keeping track of it on a daily basis. They're also quick to take shelter or hide under the bed or inside a closet at the slightest sign of lightning or thunder. Some of them are so convinced that they will get struck by lightning when they go out that they're petrified of leaving their homes in times of bad weather.

If this sounds like you, then you can start treating your astraphobia with CBT by:

- Use biofeedback to recognize your fear responses. Be aware of your heart beat, breathing, and muscle tension so you'll know when you're starting to feel anxious.
- Then, moderate this anxiety using relaxation techniques like the ones I've mentioned earlier (yoga, meditation, breathing exercises).

- Calm yourself with deep breaths and clear your mind. Think of happy, positive thoughts and listen to some soothing music while closing your eyes.
- Let your emotions wash over you and detach yourself from them. Reassure yourself that you are safe and there's nothing to be afraid of.
- Psychoeducation is also good for treating specific phobias, so educate yourself on your condition so that you can better understand what it is and how to treat it.
- Learn as much as you can about astraphobia by researching it or talking to others who have it.

Doing all of these will give you more insight into yourself and your condition, and reestablish your sense of control in your life, which will improve your psychological well-being.

Trypanophobia

Similar to cynophobia, it's typical for children to be afraid of needles and injections, but over time, their fear should diminish as they mature. However, people with trypanophobia (fear of injections) still become paralyzed at the sight of needles and allow their anxiety to rule their lives. They wrongly believe that there's no need to treat their condition and simply resort to avoiding hospitals, doctors, and any medical procedures all together. This leads them to neglect their personal health, however, and may lead to some greater problems down the road.

That being said, those with milder trypanophobia are able to get injections, but they usually feel extreme dread, worry, and sometimes even pass out or have a panic attack because of it. No matter the severity of your condition, it's essential to your psychological health and personal well-being that you treat your trypanophobia.

Common ways to treat trypanophobia include: exposure and desensitization therapy, cognitive therapy, and mindfulness training. Mindfulness training is a cognitive strategy that enables a person to bring attention to their present and fully inhabit the moment they are living in. It's a good way to treat phobias because it stops the person from overthinking and becoming overwhelmed with their fears.

- In using mindfulness to treat trypanophobia, you first need to find a safe, quiet space for you to relax in.
- Sit quietly, close your eyes, and focus on your breathing.
- If you have a mantra (like "I am brave, I am fearless"), then repeat it to yourself silently.
- Focus on the stillness of your surroundings.
- Calm yourself by listening to your heart beat.

- Identify the emotions you feel upon seeing an injection or being injected without labeling them as good or bad.
- Detach yourself from these emotions and look at them objectively. Analyze if they are really reasonable or justified.

With mindfulness training, you're better able to control your emotional responses and regulate your fear. Being aware of your condition and how irrational it is will help you regain control over your thoughts, feelings, and behaviors towards injections.

Mysophobia

Everyone knows what a neat freak is, and chances are, most people have encountered one or two in their lives before. While most "neat freaks" often get teased for liking to tidy up after themselves and organizing everything all the time, more often than not, they are wrongly labelled as obsessive-compulsive germaphobes. In fact, most people probably don't even understand what a germaphobe really is, because if they did then they'd know it's not something you should joke about.

The proper term for it is actually mysophobia (fear of germs and dirt). Mysophobia is characterized by an obsessive fear of contamination in the form of illnesses, dirt, body fluids, or bacteria. Because the problem is rooted in a person's misappraisal of the danger posed by a feared stimulus, Cognitive-Behavioral Therapy

(CBT) is really effective in treating mysophobia and has been the psychosocial intervention of choice for most cases.

As I've already explained exposure and sensitization therapy, socratic questioning, psychoeducation, and mindfulness training (all of which are common CBT techniques applied here), I think it's best if I introduce to you another useful strategy: Eye Movement Desensitization and Reprocessing (EMDR).

EMDR is particularly effective if your specific phobia is rooted in a traumatic experience from the past, because it's a therapeutic technique specially designed to treat the anxiety and distress caused by a certain memory. EMDR is all about working through your trauma and reconditioning yourself to respond to the feared stimulus in a different way (much like Exposure and Desensitization Therapy).

- The first step to using EMDR to treat mysophobia is to recall the specific traumatic event, your most painful memory regarding your mysophobia, and your most recent memory of an encounter you had with germs and bacteria.
- Then, you will need to imagine yourself in the future and picture yourself interacting with the germs or bacteria in non-fearful way (this is called a "positive cognition" with a "future template").

- Afterwards, you will need to picture yourself in that very same scenario, but this time, allow yourself to be afraid.
- As your terror and dread starts to resurface, focus on them and slowly put your hands on your upper forearms, making an X with your arms, and give yourself a hug.
- Close your eyes and gently tap your shoulders to calm yourself down.
- Go to your happy place in your mind and keep tapping yourself until your anxiety subsides.

This is called the "butterfly hug", which is a EMDR technique known as dual attention stimulation (DAS). It works by conditioning your mind to associate the feared stimulus with the calm and positive energy to transform your previously anxious and terrified state. There are many other EMDR techniques, but of the few of them that you can administer to yourself at home, the butterfly hug is by far the easiest, most popular, and most effective one.

So while specific phobias are among the most widespread of mental and emotional problems today, they are also one of the most successful and easy to treat, especially with CBT. Some of therapeutic techniques I've mentioned here, like Exposure and Desensitization Therapy, Socratic Questioning, Mindfulness Training, and EMDR, are just a few of the many different options to choose from.

Each technique has its own strengths and weaknesses, and may be suited to some cases more than others. For example, if your phobia developed as a result of a traumatic experience, then EMDR will work for you; whereas a more general phobia could benefit from EDT or mindfulness training. However, all the aforementioned techniques are founded on the same principle: they aim to help correct your anxiety-evoking misconceptions and reduce your avoidant behaviors towards the feared stimulus so you can overcome your specific phobia.

With that said, the only person who can tell you what's best for you is yourself, because no one knows what you're going through better than you do. Although it's ideal, you don't need a professional therapist's opinion or help in treating your fears and phobias with CBT, as I've already taught you a number of different ways you can safely administer treatment to yourself. All you need to do is persevere and motivate yourself enough so you can successfully manage and eliminate your phobia.

Chapter 6: CBT And OCD

How to Use CBT For Obsession and OCD

We have touched on this somewhat in the earlier chapters, but I felt that this needed more space to give it its fair due. In recent times, OCD has become somewhat of a common term amongst every day society. The word is often thrown around lightly as a tease to someone who likes things a certain way or feels the need to be orderly and tidy. Most of the people who do this, however, don't even know the first thing about OCD or how serious it actually is.

Obsessive-Compulsive Disorder (OCD) is a chronic mental illness that affects over 2.2 million people in America. It is characterized by intrusive and unsettling thoughts, images, or urges that often compel someone to engage in repetitive, ritualistic behaviors or mental acts. Understandably, those suffering from OCD feel a great deal of distress over their condition because they feel as if they are slaves to their own obsessions and compulsions. In severe cases, it can even make it difficult for the person to think about anything other than their obsessions.

Another challenge that a lot of OCD patients struggle with is overcoming their need to enact their obsessive thoughts into compulsions. OCD is driven by anxiety, and people with this disorder often wrongly believe that the only way to alleviate their anxiety is by giving into their compulsions. While it does provide some relief, it's a maladaptive solution to a much more complex problem, as it can take away an individual's sense of control and freewill over their lives.

In the early days of psychotherapy, OCD was one of the most prevalent mental disorders in the world, but most psychologists didn't have the faintest clue on how to treat it. Many of them simply resorted to psychodynamic therapy, behavioral therapy, and antidepressants, even though it was proven to have little to no significant effect. Fortunately, in 1966, psychologists discovered the first effective psychosocial intervention for OCD: exposure and ritual prevention (EX/RP).

EX/RP is a CBT technique that proved to be so successful in treating the disorder that it went on to inspire the development of other similar treatments, most of which with successful outcomes. Now, Cognitive-Behavioral Therapy (CBT) and its specialized techniques are considered the "golden standard" in treating OCD patients and alleviating their anxiety. It also helps them manage their obsessions and decrease their compulsions, which adds to a better quality of life.

So if you're suffering from OCD and looking to CBT to help you manage your condition better and ease your troubles, then you've come to the right place. In this chapter, I will be breaking down the different ways CBT can be used to treat Obsessive-Compulsive

Disorder. But first, let's go over the different kinds of obsessive thoughts and compulsions.

Among the most common obsessive thoughts include themes of:

- *Orderliness and symmetry* - people with this kind of OCD often worry about the neatness and tidiness of everything
- *Contamination* - this leads someone to fear being contaminated with germs and bacteria
- *Rumination* - this means imagining a mistake that one has done or might do
- *Checking* - this type of obsession leaves the person wondering if they've already turned off the lights, turned off the stove, locked the doors, etc.
- *Dark Thoughts* - this induces a fear of even thinking about "sinful" or evil things
- *Violence* - a person with these thoughts often fears harming others, even though he/she does not want or intend to

As for compulsive behaviors, among the major kinds are:

- *Skin-picking*
- *Hair-pulling*
- *Hoarding/collecting*
- *Repeated hand washing or cleaning*
- *Repeating particular words or phrases*
- *Performing certain tasks repeatedly*

- *Constant counting*

As you can see, OCD can have many different subtypes and symptoms, depending on the particular obsessions or compulsions of the individual. But more often than not, an effective treatment for one type of OCD is actually effective for the rest as well. There is also the degree of the severity of OCD that needs to be put into consideration.

Now let's move onto the different CBT techniques that can help treat and alleviate obsessive thoughts and OCD and how to apply them into your life:

Exposure and Ritual/Response Prevention

As I mentioned earlier, Exposure and Ritual/Response Prevention (EX/RP) is actually one of the earliest CBT techniques used to treat OCD, and the first to produce successful results. As the name implies, this particular technique involves exposing the patient gradually to situations that can trigger their obsessive thoughts and compulsive behaviors.

It might seem counterintuitive, but with the help of the therapist, the patient is guided through it and taught how to respond more effectively to the situation. They are prevented from carrying out their ritualistic behaviors and forced to find new (and often better) ways of responding to the stimulus. As a result, it decrease the frequency of their compulsions and the intensity of their obsessions over time.

Now, the therapist is an integral part of the treatment process here. However, since this book is all about teaching you how to become your own therapist and administer CBT to yourself, here's how you can do it, too:

- Firstly, you will need to make a detailed description of all of your obsessions and compulsions, and then arrange them in order of least problematic to most (depending on how recurrent or distressing they are).
- Then, use this as a guide and start working on the least problematic of the bunch, as this will be the easiest to treat.
- With a particular obsession and/or compulsion in mind, try to figure out when the symptom most often occurs and what is most likely to trigger it.
- Once you know, expose yourself to this particular stimulus and avoid responding to it with a compulsion for a certain period of time.
- This can be difficult to do on your own, especially at first, so it's best to have a trusted friend help you through it until you eventually trust yourself enough to do it on your own.

To give you a better idea of how EX/RP really works, I'll use a concrete example. Let's say you have obsessive thoughts about orderliness and symmetry, which are often triggered by the sight of unclean or disorganized things. What you need to do is ask a friend to accompany you as you are exposed to certain situations where there may be unclean or disorganized things, like at someone else's house or office.

Of course, you know that you shouldn't go around touching other people's things without their permission but you feel the uncontrollable urge to tidy up after them - arrange all their pens by color or dust off all their books and stack them in a perfectly aligned pile. Try to refrain from doing this for around five minutes. Ask your friend to distract you or talk you through it. Then, when it gets easier, next time you see something dirty or cluttered, stop yourself for ten minutes, and then twenty, and then thirty...until it eventually gets easier and easier.

In time, you will stop needing someone else to keep you from acting on your compulsive behaviors. You might even stop needing to do them in the first place, because your obsessive thoughts have become so mild that they can now be easily ignored. This is especially true once you've learned how to redirect your thoughts onto something else.

Some good distractions that can help you through the "response prevention" process are: talking to a friend about something else (i.e., the weather, the news, etc.), meditating, writing down what you want to do, making plans, making lists, knitting, baking, and painting. All you need is any relaxing or leisurely activity where you do something productive. It also helps to have your friend or companion model what the appropriate behavioral response should be. In this case, it might be merely looking at the clutter and simply saying to the person, "You have a lovely home."

This works because your brain is repeatedly reinforcing that you do not need to carry out your compulsions to be rid of the anxiety brought about by your obsessions. You will come to realize that it's okay to stop giving in to them, because nothing bad actually happens when you do. On the flip side, you might have saved yourself suffering from the burst of outrage from the home owner due to the touching of his stuff without permission.

Cognitive Therapy

The next CBT technique we will be talking about is Cognitive Therapy. While Exposure and Ritual/Response Prevention (EX/RP) was all about changing your dysfunctional behaviors for the better, Cognitive Therapy focuses on reframing your way of thinking. This will help you identify which thought patterns of yours cause you anxiety or stress and how to modify them.

Cognitive Therapy is all about challenging your thoughts and finding more functional ways of thinking. This includes strategies like self-talk, thought stopping, and relaxation training — all of which I will be breaking down for you. But first, let's contextualize everything with an example.

Say for instance, you're an elementary school teacher with OCD who has obsessions with violence. Sometimes you find yourself wondering, "What if I set one of my students on fire?" for no apparent reason. The thought surprises you and you feel immensely guilty about it because you worry that just thinking about the act in itself is already evil. Cognitive Therapy can help you with this using self-talk.

Self-Talk

Self-talk is a powerful tool for managing your OCD. Although you might not know it, you're constantly practicing self-talk everyday. It's that inner voice that monologues everything you do and think as you go on about your day, from the moment you wake up to the moment you go to sleep. However, in terms of Cognitive Therapy, self-talk refers to positive, encouraging affirmations that you give yourself as you interpret and process your personal experiences.

- In the scenario stated above, you can overcome the intrusive thoughts with self-talk by reminding yourself that you are not your disorder. It's your OCD that's making you think all these terrible things, and not at all a reflection of who you are as a person.
- Remind yourself that you are more than your condition. Find things about yourself that you love and show some

appreciation to your own strengths, accomplishments, and positive characteristics.

- Allow these intrusive thoughts into your mind but don't let them affect you or dictate what you do in any way at all. Simply observe them, say to yourself, "This is how I am feeling, but it's only a feeling. It doesn't control me."

- Moreover, you can try repeating a mantra like, "These thoughts do not hurt anyone. I do not want to hurt anyone. I am kind and caring and compassionate, but I have OCD and sometimes these thoughts get inside my head. Just because I think something doesn't mean I want it or agree with it. I am in control of my thoughts, not the other way around. It's okay. Everything is fine. Everything is good."

Habit Reversal Training

Habit Reversal Training or HRT is one of the most used types of behavioral therapy in treating OCD. With the name itself "Habit Reversal", it reverses the habit formed by individuals that are typically performed in certain situations and help them to overcome the urge to do it. This is also helpful in treating different behaviors caused by a variety of conditions, like Tourette's syndrome.

HRT is seen to be highly effective in helping people with unwanted behaviors or habits, such as hair pulling, tics, repetitive behaviors or nail biting. When treating OCD, it is highly recommendable to use this type of behavioral therapy since it helps them get rid of the urge to follow the OCD and minimize or possibly stop their repetitive behavior. This training is made up of five different parts that can help individuals overcome their disorder. It starts with:

Awareness Training

If you want to minimize or put an end to your behavior, it is important to know it and accept it beforehand. How can you put an end to something if you are not aware about it? Same goes with this, you can't stop your behavior if you aren't even aware of its presence. Through awareness training, individuals can pay attention to their behavior in order to work a way in diminishing it. This step allows you to figure out when you typically perform this particular behavior, what are some triggers and signs before you actually do it. Awareness training helps individuals know and understand their behavior more deeply and find out some things they never knew before.

Identifying and strategizing

This step identifies the problem in your behavior and partly continues the work you've done in the first step. Once you've identified all the triggers and urges you have, it is time to strategize a new behavior or a way to combat your urge. This new behavior will replace the old one. It is important to practice this new behavior and be aware. Whenever you want to go back to the old behavior you have been so used to, you can try to do this instead. For example, if your typical behavior in response to nerve-racking situations is by biting your nails, the new behavior you'll have to do is to purse your lips instead.

Finding your own motivation and sticking with your plan

When doing something difficult, we tend to find a source of motivation to keep us doing or to remind us why we're here in the first place. Same goes with habit reversal therapy, there will be some instances where you'll question what you're doing or why you're even doing it in the first place. This is why you need to write down a list of all the reasons why you want to go through HRT and make this a source of your motivation. Find all the people you want to do this for and all the problems that you've had because of your unwanted behavior. After finding you motivation, it is important to stick with your HRT and try to comply with it until the very end.

Reducing and Relaxing

These unwanted behaviors tend to show up whenever a person's body is put under a great amount of stress. So, it is important to reduce your stress level and eliminate any triggers that may induce your tics. Relax your body more and give it enough time to rest. In this part, it is important to know different relaxation techniques. There are some that also coincide with the CBT techniques such as deep breathing exercises, progression muscle relaxation, mindfulness meditation and the like.

Testing and Training

After all the different processes you've went through, it's time to test out and practice your new skills and behavior and see how you respond to different situations. You may be placed in front of triggers and it is important to train yourself to get rid of the urge to go back to your old habits. This is the most crucial step of all because it displays all the work you've done in the past. Once you've practiced this new behavior enough, it will soon become an automatic response for you and successfully replacing the old behavior you once developed.

These steps can help individuals overcome their unwanted tics. With a little effort and concentration they can possibly get through and develop a new behavior. Here is a situation example for deeper understanding.

An individual has OCD and tends to bite their nails off whenever they're under stress. So, to overcome this unwanted behavior, they have to become aware of their habit and understand it. Afterwards, they need to find a different behavior to replace that, let's say pursing their lips. When this is done, they need to practice this behavior until they get used and more accustomed to it. HRT can be done on your own. However, it is still more advisable to seek professional help in order to fully eliminate your old behavior.

Imaginal Exposure (IE)

OCD is a complex and wide psychological problem. With a lot of different types and subtypes, it can be difficult to assume which treatment is best for each one of them. There are some treatments that require a lot more intensive procedures than others. There are also others that cannot be applicable for some. Let's look at Exposure and Response Therapy for example. This type of therapy can be applicable for people who have OCD about physical things like about getting germs from touching a doorknob. The simple ERT procedure would be to let them touch multiple doorknobs without letting them wash their hands. However, it cannot be applicable for individuals who have more complex OCD behaviors. For example, individuals who are afraid of losing loved ones cannot perform ERT. So, as a substitute for this, they can undergo Imaginal Exposure or IE. Through IE, individuals will experience visualization of different scenarios that expose them to their fears or OCD. Imaginal Exposure will expose them to seemingly real-life situations and train them on how to react to these particular situations.

Imaginal Exposure is for more complex and hard to handle OCD problems. There are some who opt to go through visualizing different scenarios while others choose to write imaginal exposure stories. Through visualization, patients are asked to undergo this process:

- Think of a particular situation that triggers your OCD (like losing the ones you love)
- Once you've identified the situation, start imagining yourself in the scenario (you may be facing it by standing or looking at it)
- Afterwards, try to picture that specific scenario over and over again until it will not induce any visible or emotional trigger in you
- After being exposed to it several times, try your best to come back to that scenario until you can accept that it isn't reality and it will not always be like that.

This will reduce your negative emotions and change
your behavior towards different circumstances

Through visualization, individuals can easily access their minds and visualize their OCD triggers. By confronting their worst fears, they can slowly diminish their level of anxiety and reduce the intensity of their emotions.

There is also another way to use Imaginal Exposure and that is through writing imaginative stories. These stories entail your greatest fear and you finding a way to confront these emotions. Through writing your fears, you can let out everything you feel and expose yourself to the different OCD triggers within you. The short story that the individual will write will consist of their obsessive thoughts taken to the worst case scenario. Individuals with OCD may not be too keen to begin or go through with this type of therapy. However, it can be very crucial in allowing them to overcome their greatest fears and face their negative thoughts once and for all.

Here are some tips on how to write your own imaginal exposure short story to get the best results and to really impact your thoughts, emotions and behaviors:

Make Your Story From Your Perspective

As you are trying to overcome your own fear, it is important to write things from a first person point of view. This is so that we will actually feel the things we "did" in the story and keep it as close to our heart as much as possible. This will allow the writer to see the consequences of their action and actually feel the story. In the cognitive aspect, the brain will process the information as if it was their own doing, therefore making the therapy effective.

Always keep it realistic

It is important to not go beyond the bar. There is a fine line between reality and imagination so it's important that you should not go beyond that line. Keep things around the aspects that you think may happen if ever you would do a certain act. Don't go far from the actual topic and try to keep things as realistic as possible.

Use Authenticity

Be authentic about the thoughts you're currently thinking about and the emotions you're currently feeling. Only talk about the things that are bothering you. If it isn't actually a problem, then don't bother to write about it.

Focus on the now and write in present tense

Write your story in the present tense so that you'll actually feel you're living in it, in the exact same moment. Don't go and write about it like it happened a year ago, write things as if they are fresh and currently happening as we speak.

Keep it concise

When writing, it is important not to beat around the bush. Keep things as short and concise as possible. If it isn't actually important, then don't bother to write about it. Don't waste your time writing about things that doesn't actually keep you up at night. Rather, focus on things which detail the most important and vital part of your illness. Of course, for those with a flair for the language, it is alright to give free rein to your creative expression. Just stay on point while doing it.

Go the limit

Take your fear to the worst possible scenario. Make it out to be the worst thing that could every happen to you in your entire life. In this way, you can become exposed to the worst things and learn how to cope situations like this, or maybe even lighter ones.

Imaginal exposure can be of great use for individuals who cannot undergo ERT. It can also be extremely helpful for OCD since it exposes them to different made-up scenarios that also resemble real-life situations. Through IE, individuals can touch on both their cognitive and behavioral aspect which will in turn produce positive thoughts and better behavior.

Chapter 7: CBT And Those Bad Habits

How To Use CBT For Bad Habits

Everyone has a bad habit; something they know isn't good for them but they can't help but do anyway. However, no matter how much enjoyment we may think we feel from these bad habits — whether it's swearing, spending too much, or drinking too much coffee — we understand that they're called bad habits for a reason.

These maladaptive behaviors disrupt our lives and often make us feel like we don't have any control over ourselves, especially when they get out of hand. They hinder you from attaining your goals and jeopardize your physical and mental health. Not to mention, they're also often a waste of time and energy.

So if you came to this book looking to break a bad habit using CBT, then you're in luck. We've listed down below some of the most common bad habits and how to overcome them using different CBT techniques.

Stress Eating

Everyone feels stress from time to time, and most of us often deal with it in our own ways. Some common ways to de-stress include exercising, dancing, gardening, baking, painting, journaling, or listening to music.

However, sometimes people find comfort in eating when they're stressed, which can quickly become problematic if left unchecked. This maladaptive behavior is called "stress eating", which refers to the compulsive need or desire to eat large amounts of (often unhealthy) food whenever a person feels unhappy, anxious, or distressed. Think chocolate and ice cream.

Most of the time, people don't stress eat because they are physically hungry, but rather, because they feel momentary happiness and relief from their emotional emptiness and distress. However, this relief is fleeting and can often leave the person feeling guilty, disgusted, or hating themselves instead in the aftermath. This emotional dependency on food can have a negative effect on your body and weight, as it often results in an overwhelming sense of guilt, nausea, and obesity.

Fortunately, Cognitive-Behavioral Therapy can help with those struggling to break this vicious cycle of stress eating. Most commonly, the CBT technique applicable to treating it include journaling, which we will flesh out below to let you have an idea of how to actually go about doing it.

- Reflect on your stress eating and try to figure out what triggers it.

- Avoid these triggers at all costs.
- Keep a food journal so you can keep track of your diet. Record everything you eat in this journal and monitor your caloric intake.
- Regularly read this journal and assess your patterns of problematic eating.
- Then, with the knowledge you have gathered in your food journal, figure out how you can overcome these triggers. For example:

If you tend to stress eat the most when you are bored, keep yourself busy. Find a new hobby (i.e., exercising, origami, writing poetry) and devote your time to mastering it.

If you stress eat the most after a hard day of work, find other ways to decompress. Do yoga, drink some tea, watch a movie, take a walk, have a drink with a friend, or play with your dog. Understand that there are better, much healthier ways of relieving your stress.

If you stress eat when you're feeling down or depressed, look for other outlets to deal with your sadness. You could try talking to a friend, spending time with your loved ones, journaling how you feel, or even crying it out.

Watching Too Much TV

Television has been called "junk food for your brain", and perhaps for good reason too. Most of us have probably adopted the bad habit of watching too much TV at some point in our lives. While it may seem relaxing and enjoyable at first, it can turn into an incredible waste of your time if done in excess. It's okay to do it every once in awhile, especially after you've had a long hard week and want to kick back and reward yourself with a few episodes of your favorite show, but mindlessly consuming too much entertainment and staying on your couch all day to channel surf is actually very bad for your brain.

Numerous studies have shown that people who watch more than 3 hours of TV a day often neglect their personal health, hardly exercise at all, feel unmotivated in life, and find it hard to do anything productive or enjoyable. They've reached that certain point where watching TV no longer gives them any enjoyment or engagement at all, so why do they find it hard to stop thoughtlessly pressing the remote and just zoning out in front of their televisions?

Some believe that it's because watching TV is simple, easy to do, and requires little to no mental effort at all. Others say that it's because television gives them a false sense of connection when they're lonely or bored. Whatever the reason may be, if you're struggling to break your bad habit of watching too much TV, you can try using CBT techniques like activity scheduling and systematic positive reinforcement to help you quit.

Just follow these simple steps and reclaim your life from your addiction to TV:

- Set a certain amount of time for you to watch TV, and then do your best to stick to it.
- Then, once you're done, schedule activities for yourself to do. It can be something as simple as doing the chores or your homework, as long as you do something other than watch TV all day.
- Then, as the days go by, lessen your time in front of the TV and schedule more and more activities for yourself.
- Gradually increase the level of difficulty or time for your activities, like going from washing the dishes, to baking brownies, to hanging out with your friends. (yes, for some folks who have watched too much tv, interacting with actual living humans may seem to be a herculean task)
- Every time you complete a certain task or activity, reward yourself with something other than watching television.

These techniques work because they teach your brain to associate the positive feelings you get from your rewards with not watching TV. Gradually cutting it out of your life also helps to make you feel less withdrawal symptoms and more of a certain sense of purpose in your recovery process.

Procrastinating

Everyone's tried procrastinating from time to time. If you don't know, procrastinating means putting off something you often don't want to do but need to, and leaving it at the very last minute. However, while you're out there enjoying yourself and distracting your mind, trying to forget about all the work you need to do, deep down inside, you're feeling bad and there's a constant sense of guilt hanging over your head.

If you turn procrastination into a habit, you will suffer from diminished performance, poorer mental and physical health, and more feelings of stress, worry, and guilt over time. Procrastination is a maladaptive, self-defeating behavior that gives you short-term benefits but at a pricier, long-term cost. So why do so many of us procrastinate anyway? And why is it so hard to stop?

Some researchers theorize that people procrastinate because they wrongly believe it to be a form of "self-care"; while others believe that we've learned to procrastinate from our role models; and some say that we procrastinate because of a deep-seated fear of failing and feeling like we're not good enough to do the tasks which we are supposed to do. Because there are so many different reasons why we procrastinate, there are also a variety of different ways you can stop doing it. Examples include:

- Practice positive self-talk. Tell yourself something like, "I know it's hard, but we have to do it. So please, let's just start it. I believe in you. You're going to do great."

- Find new role models you can look up to, who do everything on time. Follow them around for a while and ask them to help you understand why it's so much better not to procrastinate.

- Develop your skills. Whatever it is you're putting off, if you feel insecure and unsure of yourself and think you won't be able to do it well, then work on your skills. This will boost your self-confidence and motivate you to procrastinate less and do better at the task.

Choosing Bad Partners/Relationships

Everyone knows what a "bad relationship" is. It's the kind of relationship where you don't feel valued or heard, where your partner doesn't treat you as an equal. This can mean that they're unfaithful to you, or they feel embarrassed to be seen with you, or that they only ever want to talk and never listen. Sometimes, bad relationships mean unrequited love; being with a partner whom you love but doesn't love you back. Whatever kind of bad relationship you've been in, the end result is always the same: you feel heartbroken and hating yourself for being so stupid.

If you've had a string of bad relationships like the ones I just described, then perhaps it's because you have a bad habit of choosing the wrong partner. Oftentimes, this stems from an attraction towards people you can't have or don't reciprocate your feelings, either to the same degree or at all. Author Stephen Chbosky once wrote, "We accept the love we think we deserve," and this is exactly why some people constantly find themselves in one bad relationship after another.

If that person is you and you're looking to change your self-defeating ways, then some Cognitive-Behavioral Therapy (CBT) can help you with that. Your goal here should be towards building your self-esteem and developing a more positive relationship with yourself, which you can do through journaling, positive self-talk, and mindfulness training.

- Write down at least ten things about yourself that you love. It can be either personality traits or physical features, as long as it is positive.
- Now, read out loud these positive statements to yourself, and afterwards, try to add some more.
- Whenever you're feeling down about yourself, say something positive like, "I know you can get through this, you're strong," or "Just because other people can't see your worth doesn't mean you don't have any. I love you. I think you're amazing."
- It also helps to start each day with positivity, so write down these messages on your wall beside your bed

or somewhere you can see when you wake up. (try the toilet wall mirror too, you can look at it every single day when you brush your teeth)

- Then, set aside 10-20 minutes each day for you to meditate. Recall your day as you're meditating and try to identify the emotions you've felt.
- Ask yourself why you felt that way and if it was reasonable or justified.
- If ever you did something wrong or embarrassing, forgive yourself.
- Get comfortable being alone for now. Learn to enjoy your own company.

All you need to overcome your self-defeating habit of being in bad relationships is really to just practice more self-love and boost your self-esteem. Once you do that, you will start choosing partners who are right for you and stay in healthier relationships.

So all in all, while bad habits may not seem like the most pressing of psychological problems, they still need to be addressed. Little things like watching too much TV can quickly turn into TV addiction and, before you know it, you've wasted months or years off of your life just by staying in the couch all day, unable to let go of the remote.

Procrastination is also particularly harmful to students or anyone with a demanding job that requires them to give it their all. It can significantly impede their performance and cost them a lot of great opportunities in life, as well as lower the quality and standard of their work, which will give others a bad impression of them.

There are lots of other bad habits that we didn't mention here, but a lot of the same techniques we've detailed above can be applied to quite a number of them. Cognitive-Behavioral Therapy can help you break the vicious cycle of wasting your time with unproductive things by reconditioning your mind and changing your maladaptive behaviors.

Chapter 8: A Little Bit Of Structure
And Hand Holding Never Hurt Anyone

The 21-Day Step-by-Step Guide

Now that we've wrapped up our discussion on all the major problems and issues Cognitive-Behavioral Therapy (CBT) and its many techniques can deal with, it's time to apply all that knowledge on how to solve your particular problem in mind.

If the issues you are dealing with right now weren't covered in the earlier chapters, don't worry. I've created this comprehensive, 21-day step-by-step guide on how you can deal with almost any difficult situation using CBT and come out the other end a better, happier, and more emotionally well-balanced person. Be guided by these steps and keep them in mind on your journey to mental wellness with CBT.

- **Day 01 - Know what your problems are**

  Before anything else, you need to sit yourself down and figure out what it is you've been struggling with lately. Get a pen and paper or make a list in your journal about all the problems bothering you right now. No matter how big or small, write down every single problem you're experiencing that you can think of.

- **Day 02 - Sorting out your priorities**

Next, what you should do is look through your list and figure out for yourself which problems are causing you the most distress. Rank them from most difficult to deal with to the least, and from there, start with the last entry on your list. This way, you start with the easiest challenge and work your way up over time, as you gain more understanding and better mastery over how to use CBT.

- **Day 03 - Understanding the problem**

Now, with a particular problem in mind, focus on that and devote all your attention to understanding it. This stage of the process is known as guided discovery. A common CBT and counselling technique, guided discovery is all about reflecting on how you process information.

So go through the problem in your mind and try to recall how it came about and the ways in which you responded to it. Understand as much as you can about what caused the problem and what is perpetuating it. Consider the situational, social, mental, emotional, and behavioral factors involved.

- **Day 04 - Identifying your obstacles**

Following that same train of thought as the last point, identify the obstacles getting in the way of your path to mental wellness. Think of all the things that make it harder for you to resolve your particular problem and brainstorm ways in which you can overcome these obstacles. This is a crucial step in the process because if you overlook this or fail to do it, then it will simply keep coming back to haunt you and hinder your progress every step of the way.

- **Day 05 - Set goals for yourself**

Now that there's nothing getting in the way of you resolving your problem anymore, it's time for you to set goals for yourself. Know what it is that you want to achieve and break it down into simpler, more manageable goals. For example, if you want to quit smoking, then smoke 1 less cigarette than your usual today, and then 2 the next day, and then 5, and then 10...until eventually, you quit smoking all together. Remember you have to walk a tight line between setting unassailable goals and goals which are too lax. The goal has to be achievable at each given state of your being. Referencing to the cigarette example, smoking one less cigarette than you usual could be deemed as achievable in your present circumstance, while asking you to jump from smoking daily to totally cutting out smoking immediately would be deemed as one of the unassailable goals I was talking about. Progression from cutting one cigarette to two and more, would entail you having to be honest with yourself and go about setting challenging but achievable goals.

- **Day 06 - Figure out your thoughts on the problem**

Take your journal out again and write down every single thought you have regarding this particular problem. How does it make you feel? What are the beliefs and assumptions you have surrounding it? Does it affect the way you feel about yourself or your life? Be as honest as possible with yourself and really take the time to ruminate on these questions.

- **Day 07 - Identify your automatic thoughts**

As I mentioned before in the introduction of this book, automatic thoughts refer to the thoughts that occur in response to a certain trigger or event. These are reflexive and unconsciously done, but can greatly impact a person's life. So whenever something happens to you — no matter how big or small — quickly write down or record the first thought that pops into your head.

- **Day 08 - Practice more positive thinking**

Here you can use cognitive restructuring to recondition your brain and change those negative automatic thoughts into more positive ones. Similar to guided discovery, cognitive restructuring will allow you to change the way you process information because it asks you to challenge your thoughts and the emotions and behaviors that they elicit. Once you've identified the unfavorable thought, try to change it in a way that finds a positive aspect in it.

For example, if you think to yourself, "Nobody likes me," you need to challenge it by thinking about all the people who actually do like you. Afterwards, you can think about all the reasons why you don't need people to like you. So now, every time this negative thought pops into your head, challenge it with "These people like me," and "I don't need others to like me, because I already like myself."

- **Day 09 - Reaffirm yourself**

Self-affirmations can help enhance your likelihood of succeeding in resolving your problem with CBT by boosting your self-esteem and increasing your motivation. I've already talked about it a lot, especially in dealing with anxiety, depression, and OCD, but the change that it can have on your life really is astounding. If practiced daily and devotedly, these positive statements are powerful enough to change the way you feel about yourself and the world for the better, along with minimizing your anxiety, stress, and negative thinking.

I've shared several affirmations and positive mantras you can speak to yourself in those chapters I mentioned before, but you can also make one for yourself! Just be positive and strive to see yourself and your situation in the best possible light you can.

- **Day 10 - Know how you feel about the problem**

Practice mindfulness when thinking about the problem at hand. Describe the situation and how you feel about it. Go into detail about the things it made you think and the way it made you feel. What was the first thought that popped into your mind? How did you feel? Identify these emotions and refrain from labelling them as "good" or "bad" and reacting to them in anyway at all.

- **Day 11 - Manage your emotions**

Now that you've already dealt with your problematic thought patterns, it's time to move on to your negative emotions. Do some more reflection and ponder on what certain situations or objects trigger unwanted emotions in you, and until you figure out why, try to avoid them at all costs. Keep your emotions in check by practicing meditation or other relaxation techniques like breathing exercises and yoga.

- **Day 12 - Overcome your negative emotions**

Next, you need to work on overcoming whatever negative emotions you might have. Sadness, stress, doubt, jealousy, shame, frustration, or guilt, positive self-talk can help you deal with it. Like I previously mentioned in the chapter about OCD, positive self-talk is a powerful tool in working through your negative emotions.

Simply reassure yourself that everything is fine and well, and think of as many reasons as you can to support that claim. You don't need to resort to lying to yourself; just practice genuine gratitude for all the good things in your life and remind yourself of all the great things about you.

- **Day 13 - Overcome your fears**

This step is optional, but if your fear is a big part of your problem, then you need to deal with it correctly. The techniques I've mentioned in the chapter about specific phobias can all be applied to resolve just about any fear you might have, so give it a try. You could use graded exposure, relaxation training, mindfulness training, socratic questioning, psychoeducation, and even EMDR if the fear is especially traumatic.

- **Day 14 - Identify your maladapative behaviors**

After you've addressed the dysfunctional patterns in your thoughts and emotions, let's proceed to your maladaptive behaviors. Sit yourself down again and reflect on all the habits and behavioral responses that you feel are bad for you and want to stop doing. Write it all down in your journal. It could be something like lying, sleeping in, saying sorry all the time, procrastinating, and so on.

- **Day 15 - Overcome these negative behaviors**

Once you've already identified the negative behavior you would like to stop doing, the next step is to overcome it. You can use aversive conditioning, wherein you pair the behavior with an aversive stimulus to recondition your brain into no longer wanting to do it. One common example of this would be flicking your wrist with a rubber band every time you say something mean or rude.

You can follow the steps listed in the chapter dealing with bad habits and behaviors. They would be helpful in shoring up the resolve to overcome these negative aspects, while at the same time emphasizing on the positive steps which you are taking.

- **Day 16 - Replace them with positive behaviors**

Now that you've successfully rid yourself of those maladaptive behaviors, it's time to replace them with more positive ones through systematic positive reinforcement (SPR). Applying the same principles of behavior as aversive conditioning, SPR works by rewarding yourself with something every time you do something positive.

For example, buying yourself some ice cream every time you overcome your fear of public speaking or do well on a test. This will encourage you to keep doing those positive behaviors more and more over time, even when the reward is no longer there, because your brain has already learned to associate it with those positive feelings.

- **Day 17 - Accept the things you can't change**

  But what if there are certain things about your problem that you can't resolve or that you have no control over? For example, in dealing with a breakup or being rejected for a job or college that you want, a lot of the situation is largely out of your control. The best thing for you to do would be to simply accept it and come to terms with it.

  Doing meditation as well as in depth mindfulness training can really be of help when faced with situations that seem to be totally out of your control. As they always like to say, change is the only constant and the only thing you can control is yourself.

- **Day 18 - Work through any past trauma**

  At this point of the process, your journey should be coming to a close. You've resolved all your dysfunctional thoughts and behaviors, and learned to control your emotions better. However, if there is still some lingering trauma from your past regarding the problem, then you need to deal with it as well.

  It might be that you need to forgive someone who hurt you or come to terms with yourself about the things you did or didn't do. If your trauma runs deeper than this, you might want to try EMDR, the therapeutic treatment we've mentioned in treating specific phobias like mysophobia.

- **Day 19 - Be proud of all the progress you've made**

  As our journey is nearing its end, it's important that you take the time to look back on all the progress you've made and feel proud of how far you've come. It was certainly a struggle, but you've made it. You've done your best and now you're ready to move on from your problems. Pat yourself on the back. You deserve it.

- **Day 20 - Ending treatment & maintaining change** (tips from Chapter 8)

  Now it's finally time to end your treatment and close this chapter of your life. The problem that made you seek this book for help is now resolved, and all that's left for you to do is go on with your life and continue to be the better person that you are. While the hardest part is certainly over, you need to work hard to keep going and do your best not to fall back on your old, dysfunctional ways. Maintain the positive change in your life by following the tips I've listed down below, later on in this chapter.

- **Day 21 - Apply what you've learned**

  As the famous American pastor Joel Osteen once said, "Every day, we have plenty of opportunities to get angry, stressed or offended. But what you're doing when you indulge in these negative emotions is giving something outside of yourself power over your happiness. You can choose not to let little things upset you."

Bearing in mind those wise words, all of the things you've learned and the progress you've made would be useless if you didn't apply it to your life. Your journey with CBT has been all about learning to be your own therapist, so use all the skills you've developed and knowledge you've gathered from this book and apply it to whatever challenges you face next. The more you cultivate it, the easier it will be to apply, and the better your life will be.

Other Ways You Can Live Your Best Life

Along with this 21-day step-by-step guide, there are plenty of other positive habits and practices you can incorporate into your every day routine to improve the overall quality of your life. This is ideal because it reinforces your learnings and sees to it that even when you're done with the program, everything you've worked hard on and all the progress you've made still stays with you. A few additional ways you can continue living your best life is through:

1. Meditation

We've said it time and time again: meditation is good for your mental and emotional health. An integral facet of relaxation training, which is used to treat anxiety, obsessive thoughts, OCD, phobias, and maladaptive behaviors, meditation in and of itself can be greatly beneficial.

Just in case you needed reminding, meditation helps relieve your stress, facilitates better sleep, reduces muscle tension and body pain, reduces blood pressure, boosts your immune system, deals with your worries and anxieties, clears your mind, increases positive emotions, and promotes greater focus, awareness, and emotional control.

Millions of people from all over the world attest to how practicing meditation daily has changed their lives for the better, so why not do the same? Set aside 10-20 minutes a day to meditate and sit in tranquil silence. Find a comfortable, safe space - be it, in your room or on your bed - and set your timer. From the moment it starts ticking to the moment it stops, try to think about nothing but your breathing. Get to work on identifying your emotions and releasing all the negativity you feel. Find some peace of mind, and when you're done, go on about your day with a better, more rational mindset.

2. Nature Therapy

If you feel that sitting in silence for a few minutes a day and doing seemingly nothing is really not for you, then nature therapy is a good alternative you can try. Nature therapy (sometimes also known as "eco therapy") is all about reconnecting with Mother Nature. It is founded on the belief that all human beings are a part of the circle of life here on Earth and that our souls all yearn to be at peace with our natural environments.

Doesn't it feel good to go outside, breathe in the fresh air and bask in the sunshine? Don't you feel a certain serenity wash over you when you enjoy the beauty of the great outdoors? In the modern age of technology where humans have become more urbanized and screen-driven than ever, nature therapy provides a calming, therapeutic effect because it reminds us of place in the natural world. Practicing nature therapy can give you a sense of balance and harmony in your life.

So make time in your busy schedule to spend a day at the beach, go camping in the woods, or take a weekend trip to the lakehouse or golf course. Leave behind all your worries and stresses for the day, and your emotional and mental wellbeing will be all the better for it.

On the other hand, even if you live in a bustling city and work a strenuous job you just can't leave behind, you can still find the beauty in nature in small ways — like going for a walk in the park or tending to your garden in the backyard. Anything that gets you outdoors and brings a sense of purpose-ness to your experience is already nature therapy in and of itself.

3. Stargazing

Similar to nature therapy, stargazing has also been found to be very therapeutic to our mental health, perhaps because it satisfies our innate human need for connection and meaning in life. Looking up at all the vastness and beauty of the inky, black night sky and its twinkling stars reminds us that we are not alone in the Universe; we are all living on the same cosmic plane, under the same beautiful sky.

Even the ancient Greeks as early as 750 B.C. gazed up at the stars and looked to the night sky for guidance. When it's just you and the stars, time seems to stand still. You'll find that your thoughts tend to clear and your connection with the world around you strengthens. It can make you feel imaginative, inspired; or calm, hopeful, and at peace with yourself and the world.

With that said, it's important that you go out on your roof or look out your balcony window every once and a while to marvel at the night sky, because it can do a lot to help you find peace in your life and give you a new perspective. It helps you slow down every now and then and contemplate the greater meaning of life. When you're with others, it also provides the ideal ambiance for having deep, meaningful conversations and making great memories.

4. Physical Activity

Next, another way you can improve your life — and perhaps the most obvious of all the ones listed here — is by becoming more physically active. For those of you out there already rolling your eyes and hating the thought, I implore you to listen: you don't have to go to the gym every day, but regularly engaging in exercise and making sure you work up a sweat every other day or so will do wonders for your physical, mental, and emotional health. This is especially important if you work a desk job or have a sedentary lifestyle.

Some alternatives to working out at the gym include: jogging, biking, swimming, dancing, boxing, hot yoga, wall climbing, horse riding, gymnastics, or playing a sport like basketball, football, soccer, badminton, tennis, volleyball, field hockey, or even fencing. There are so many other ways you can get active and take care of your body; choosing the right one for you is all a matter of what you enjoy and whether you'd like to develop your stamina, strength, flexibility, or coordination.

We all know that exercise is good for you, because it keeps your muscles working, burns calories, and allows us to release toxins from our body in the form of sweat. Aside from that, exercise also releases endorphins in our brain, which create positive feelings and help us feel less pain. It also relieves feelings of depression, anxiety, and stress, as well as promote muscle growth and bone strengthening. It boosts your energy, clears your skin, fights against antioxidants, and minimizes the risk of chronic illness. It's also been shown to help you relax more and sleep better, which brings us to our next point.

5. Better Sleep

Getting a good night's sleep does a lot to improve a person's overall functioning. Most adults need 7-9 hours of sleep every night, but the quality of sleep that they're getting matters, too. Sleep promotes better heart health and better blood flow. It reduces stress, makes you more energized and alert, improves your memory, facilitates weight loss, enhances the collagen in your skin, and allows your body and your organs to repair itself.

However, not getting the needed amount or quality of sleep on a regular basis puts a person more at risk of developing depression, heart disease, diabetes, and even certain cancers. It weakens your immune system, impairs your cognitive functions (i.e., memory, decision-making, reasoning, problem solving), promotes wrinkles, and lowers your metabolism. So it's not hard to see why you need to make sure your body is getting the amount and quality of sleep that it deserves.

You can do this is by improving your sleep hygiene. Try to go to sleep and wake up at the same time every day, to regulate your body clock. Resist the urge to sleep in and stick to a strict sleep schedule. It's also good to have a nightly routine of things to do before you go to bed, like reading, brushing your teeth, or listening to music. Put your phone away and don't look at any electronic screens like your TV or computer monitor at least 1 hour before you go to bed, because it makes it more difficult for you to fall asleep. For the same reason, avoid drinking any caffeinated drinks like coffee or soda 3 hours before bed, and take naps between 11 AM to 3 PM for not more than one hour.

6. Healthy Eating

Finally, another way you can take better care of your mental and emotional wellbeing is by eating healthier and having a well-balanced diet. Observing proper nutrition helps a person lose weight, regulate their metabolism, fight against chronic disease, keep their heart healthy, strengthen their bones and teeth, improve their memory, and puts them in a more positive and energized mood.

Still, in spite of all these benefits, many of us still find it difficult to eat healthier because our cravings for pizza, burgers, donuts, soda, chocolate, cookies, and candy. While these foods may be delicious and addictive, they are also low in nutritional value and negatively impact our health. The first step towards change may be the hardest, but over time, it'll get easier and easier to do, and your body will thank you immensely for taking care of it.

Some tips to help you start eating healthier are: drink herbal tea instead of soft drinks or juice; have at least 1 day a week where you don't eat meat; gradually quit eating fast food; eat fresh fruits when you're craving sugar or candy; avoid food that's high in saturated fat (like pizza and burgers) or processed sugar (like milkshakes and ice cream). A nutritious diet is one of the foundations of good health — physically, mentally, and emotionally speaking — so make sure you take good care of yourself by following these tips.

Chapter 9: To Sum It Up

We've officially finished our journey together to mental and emotional wellness with Cognitive-Behavioral Therapy (CBT).

Recapping Everything

The introduction began with an explanation of why CBT is important, especially if you consider yourself a pessimistic thinker or have been struggling with negative feelings and self-destructive behaviors. I introduced CBT to you as an effective solution to your troubles and elaborated on its guiding principles, mainly: our thoughts control our emotions and behaviors.

In Chapter 1, I included a brief history of CBT and outlined how it came about and how it changed and developed throughout the years. I listed down all the major benefits you could get from letting CBT into your life, as well as all the factors to consider when deciding whether or not CBT would be the right choice for you. There were also ways on how to make the most out of CBT and this book mentioned.

Chapter 2 was all about the basic tools of CBT, wherein I discussed the importance of journalling, mindfulness meditation, behavioral activation, and affirmations, as well as a guide on how to do them.

Next, Chapter 3 introduced the 30 different ways CBT handles issues and how it could help with specific problems. It was largely devoted to dealing with many different kinds of anxiety, like GAD, social anxiety, panic disorder, and PTSD.

In Chapter 4, you learned all about how to use CBT in treating your depression. There were several techniques discussed, as well as the different kinds of depression like major depression, manic depression, perinatal, atypical depression, and situational depression.

Chapter 5 is where you learned how to use CBT to treat and eliminate fears and specific phobias, such as the fear of heights, thunder and lightning, flying, spiders, dogs, injections, and germs.

You also learned how to manage different kinds of obsessive thoughts and compulsions with CBT in Chapter 6, where techniques like EW/RP, cognitive therapy, and more were introduced.

Chapter 7 did the same, but for maladaptive behaviors. It discussed all the most common ones, like stress eating, watching too much TV, procrastinating, eating junk food, being tardy, and so on.

Once all the major areas of psychological distress and dysfunction CBT could resolve were already addressed, Chapter 8 outlined a comprehensive 21-day, step-by-step guide on how to use all the different CBT techniques into dealing with more general problems that weren't mentioned earlier. Some additional tips on how to continue improving your life even after your treatment process with CBT has ended were also discussed.

Thus, that brings us to Chapter 9, the final chapter of the book dedicated to taking stock of everything. Now that you understand the importance of CBT, its different techniques, and how to apply it in resolving your personal problems, it's time to look further into the future and ask yourself: what's next?

Life After Cognitive-Behavioral Therapy

Now that you've learned all about CBT and successfully applied it to dealing with your own personal difficulties, it's time to finally move on with your life. The hardest part is over, and what waits ahead for you is a brighter future.

Ending your therapy can be difficult, because often times people just can't believe that it's over. While some feel a sense of fulfillment or emotional closure when they're done, others don't, which can make it harder to say goodbye. However, bear in mind that just because this journey is over doesn't mean you should forever close your door on Cognitive-Behavioral Therapy. Problems are a natural part of life, and so, you can expect to apply everything you've learned here later on again in your future.

What's more, even if you don't have any problems to deal with at the moment, it's still good to practice some of these CBT techniques in taking care of your mental health. So keep journaling, keep meditating. Always think before you act and be critical of your thoughts and emotions. Unlike a lot of life's endings, ending this journey that you've had with CBT right now shouldn't be a sad one, so be happy and keep all your learnings with you as you move forward into the future.

Conclusion

And that brings us to the end of our journey together. Hopefully, you will have successfully accomplished the 21-day step-by-step program we've outlined here in the earlier chapter for you or, if I've already covered your specific problem in the chapters about anxiety, depression, OCD, and bad habits, applied some of the CBT techniques I've mentioned there.

Thank you for coming along with me on our journey with Cognitive-Behavioral Therapy. I hope you learned a lot about CBT and that it changed your life for the better. I also hope you've achieved all that you've wanted from these programs as well as techniques, and that it has helped you effectively overcome whatever struggles or challenges you were dealing with, in a healthy and functional way.

If you've followed all the steps correctly and devotedly, and integrated these additional tips we've provided on how you can keep promoting mental and emotional wellness in your life, then you should be well equipped by now to deal with whatever life throws your way next. Congratulations, and best of luck to you!

Here's to a happier and healthier you. Here's to becoming the best version of yourself and creating positive change to start living your best life today, all with the help of Cognitive-Behavioral Therapy (CBT).

Bonus Extra!

Bonus Extra On Meditation

I have also seen fit to add in this extra segment on meditation because I find that it is helpful on both a personal as well as professional level. It also acts as both a complementary, as well as an integral part of the CBT process. Alright, enough talk and let's dive in to the meat and potatoes of the matter.

Breath Meditation

The kind of meditation that I would like to talk about at this juncture would be dealing with the breath as the principal object of focus. This means when we attend to our meditation sessions, the thing that we will bring our mind and awareness to will be the simple in and out of our breath.

Why the breath?

Well, because we all have to breathe right? Somehow or another, every one probably has to breathe, either through the nose or through the mouth. Hence the breath makes for a very handy and easily accessible object of focus which we can depend upon just about any place, any time. Think about it, if you were on a plane with absolutely nothing to do, or commuting on the daily train, you can just sit or even stand comfortably and start focusing on your breath. Easy peasy.

How to do Breath Meditation

You would have to find a comfortable space for yourself. A note here. You do not have to be in the traditional meditative pose, which is most often cast as sitting cross legged on the ground and having your back erect and eyes closed. In this situation, finding a comfortable space for yourself could easily just mean getting to a less occupied area on the bus or train, your own table in the office or even doing meditation whilst standing up. (it can be done, you just need practice)

Of course, for the absolute beginner, or for just about anyone who is easily distracted by all the hum drum that life has to offer, going to a quiet spot like your home, a park, by the sea or in the mountains would be doing yourself no harm if you were looking to derive maximum benefits from meditation. For me, I would recommend that you choose somewhere that is very easily accessible. You may know a perfect spot deep in the mountains, with picturesque views and cool, fresh air. Yet if you were to only go there for one or two weeks per year tops, it really isn't some place for you to consider as the spot to do your daily meditation. Most folks would be doing it at home, or somewhere easily accessible from home.

You would want to try and ensure that it is weather proof, which means you don't have to cut short your session every time there is a rain cloud. Fresh air would be a relatively good alternative to the air conditioned air we are constantly exposed to these days. Minimize the number of bugs in your meditative space so as to cut down on the potential distractions. Try focusing while having a fly attempting to crawl up your nostril. You get the idea. Once you have the constant space settled, then we move on to the posture.

The meditative posture. To be fair, the classic cross legged sitting on the floor with your back erect and eyes closed position is really one where most meditation centers and courses would adopt. You can use that as the benchmark which you would strive to attain, but that does not have to be your starting point.

You can begin meditation by sitting comfortably on a chair, just do not slouch. You do not want to compress your stomach and intestinal areas because you might limit your air intake, which would then affect your breath and focus. You can also begin meditation by lying on your back. Some folks do it on their beds, but a word of caution. Most times, people find that they would drift off to sleep just because it is their bed. As the human body is so sensitive and conditioned to anchors and cues that by just being on the bed, the urge to sleep would automatically kick in. Meditation does not equate to sleeping. That much has to be made clear at this point. For folks who find it needful to lie down, it would be best done on a harder surface. Perhaps a wooden floor or a thin mattress laid on the ground. The firmness of the ground would reduce the tendency for the body to fall into sleep mode, though I personally would like to state here that sitting up would still be one of the better postures to be in so that you would find it easier to concentrate.

Focus on the Breath. Now with all the sundry duties settled, it is time to get down to the actual process of meditation. Your primary focus will be on your breath. You would be paying attention to your nostrils as you take in the breath, and again to your nostrils as you breathe out. Always breathe through your nose, which is another reason why sitting up is good because most folks would be able to do nose breathing whilst sitting up. You will pay attention to your nostrils expanding slightly, and the coolness of the air on the intake, and you will pay attention to your nostrils puffing out slightly, and the hotness of the breath on the exhalation. All your attention and focus should be centered on your nostrils.

During this practice, thoughts as well as images would tend to come into this personal space which we are trying to create for ourselves. It is all well and easy to just give you a simple - ignore them, but it doesn't quite work that way does it? Our primary focus is our breath, so what should we do now that images and thoughts are dragging our attention away from the breath and onto them?

At the start, you can give those thoughts and images the attention that they crave. If you start thinking about what to eat later, or what movie to watch on the weekend, you can actually allow your consciousness to pay attention to them. Try to build up your awareness such that you seem to be looking at those thoughts with a sort of detachment. It is as if you are looking at someone else's thoughts instead. You give these thoughts the attention, but you try to build up that detachment where you look at these thoughts through the lens of a third party. Then you want to watch these thoughts as they spiral away after initially demanding your focus and attention. As they fade off, you will refocus your awareness and concentration on the breath.

This focus on and focus off the breath due to the interruption from our mental thoughts would be a pretty constant occurrence in the earlier stages of meditation. Some of the learned folks would compare your mind to a monkey, and your focus on the breath as a chain tied to a stout post, which is binding the monkey. At the initial stages, the mind or monkey would jump up and down, but after exhausting its energy, there would be periods it would just lie still. Those are the times where you find yourself being able to focus on the breath for a protracted period. Just to be clear, there is no hard and fast rule to what is termed as a protracted period. It all depends on every individual. For a person who has a hyperactive mind, having five or ten seconds of focus on the breath can be termed as a protracted period.

As the meditation practice grows, you will find that the monkey tends to disturb lesser. Even during the incidences of disturbance, you would tend to be able to make it go rest in a shorter amount of time than before. With the growth of your concentration on your breath, you will find that your sessions will start to stretch. From ten minutes to twenty. From half an hour to the full hour.

During the course of the session, your entire focus will still be on your breath. There is no need to bring in any thoughts or imagery which may be troubling you.

I will not be expounding any of the benefits that breath meditation will bring, but I would rather leave it to yourself in experiencing them. As a parting word, I can say personally a calmer approach to life seems to be something which I have experienced.

To a fulfilling meditative journey. Please start.

A Way of Helping Out

At the end of this book, would you be able to think of 1 or 2 things which you have learnt and are able to share with the folks on amazon?

Please Go ahead and share that 1 best thing which you have learnt

It would be a great help to other folks in letting them know of your beneficial experience

And it would be helping me out as well because reviews mean quite a big deal

Thank You Very Much!

Printed in Great Britain
by Amazon